Home Design for Your Future

GRACIOUS LIVING

GRACIOUS LIVING

Home Design for Your Future

Naomi Neville and E. Ashley Rooney

Foreword by Dr. Jill M. Bjerke

Schiffer Publishing Ltd

4880 Lower Valley Road • Atglen, PA 19310

Other Schiffer Books by the Authors:
Barn Again, Restored and New Barns for the 21st Century. E. Ashley Rooney.
ISBN: 978-0-7643-3431-3. $34.99.

Green Homes: Dwellings for the 21st Century. E. Ashley Rooney, David Hartke, and John C. McConnell.
ISBN: 978-0-7643-3033-9. $39.99.

Retreats to Retirement. E. Ashley Rooney.
ISBN: 0-7643-2339-3. $39.95.

Spectacular Small Kitchens: Design Ideas for Urban Spaces. E. Ashley Rooney.
ISBN: 0-7643-2110-2. $19.95.

Other Schiffer Books on Related Subjects:
Alternatives to Aging. Stephen Kravette.
ISBN: 0-9149-1889-3. $14.95.

Amazing Space: Architect Designed Houses Under $300,000.
Lucy D. Rosenfeld. ISBN: 0-7643-0642-1. $39.95.

Library of Congress Control Number: 2013936098

Designed by RoS
Type set in Swis721 Th BT/News Gothic BT

ISBN: 978-0-7643-4359-9
Printed in China

Published by Schiffer Publishing, Ltd.
4880 Lower Valley Road
Atglen, PA 19310
Phone: (610) 593-1777; Fax: (610) 593-2002
E-mail: Info@schifferbooks.com

For the largest selection of fine reference books on this and related subjects, please visit our website at **www.schifferbooks.com.** You may also write for a free catalog.

This book may be purchased from the publisher.
Please try your bookstore first.

We are always looking for people to write books on new and related subjects. If you have an idea for a book, please contact us at proposals@schifferbooks.com.

Schiffer Books are available at special discounts for bulk purchases for sales promotions or premiums. Special editions, including personalized covers, corporate imprints, and excerpts can be created in large quantities for special needs. For more information contact the publisher.

In Europe, Schiffer books are distributed by
Bushwood Books
6 Marksbury Ave.
Kew Gardens
Surrey TW9 4JF England
Phone: 44 (0) 20 8392 8585; Fax: 44 (0) 20 8392 9876
E-mail: info@bushwoodbooks.co.uk
Website: www.bushwoodbooks.co.uk

CONTENTS

FOREWORD

Aging in Place with Grace

Dr. Jill M. Bjerke

The word "design" has come to represent a vast number of concepts, each with their own inherent elements. By its very definition, the purpose of design is to create a plan for executing the construction of an object, such as a building, dress, or software program. When it comes to creating a safe, well-thought out plan for constructing a home that one can live in as he/she ages, design takes on specific strategies and elements.

The entire purpose of aging in place is to retain and maintain one's independence and mobility in an environment that is safe, secure, and comfortable. The concept of aging in place (or aging at home, as it is known in Canada) is not a new one, and the term seems to have captured the hearts and minds of the entire world, as this phrase has become ubiquitous.

In actuality, it was reflected in the physical constraints that Franklin Roosevelt had to endure because of his polio. He had changes made to his "retreat" that included wider doors and hallways and lower windows so that he could look outside from his wheelchair. One could certainly infer that these alterations reflect the beginnings of the effort to maintain mobility and autonomy in one's home.

"Aging in place" used to represent different levels of services within a senior or retirement community and the idea of being able to remain in that community as your health care and other needs change is still a very popular option. Most senior residences are built to be compliant with the Americans with Disability Act (ADA), which provides special considerations for wider hallways, elevators, ramps, and other accessibility compliant features.

Now, aging in place has come to represent a residential design concept that involves certain structural and cosmetic alterations that make a home safer to reside in as we experience the natural physiological changes that take place as we age. This creates a "win-win" situation for residential housing stock as these changes can be incorporated into new construction or used to remodel existing homes, and can increase the use of a residence to a wider demographic, including those with and without mobility or other similar issues.

In 2005, Partners for Livable Community and the National Association of Area Agencies on Aging began to work with nine specific communities for the purpose of expanding programs, services, and policies that shape the age in place concept. In 2006, these same groups collaborated with the National Association of Counties and the MetLife Foundation to carry out a survey of 10,000 United States cities and counties to compile information on how needs of the aging population were being met. The subsequent result was *The Maturing of America: Getting Communities on Track for an Aging Population.* This document is significant in that it identifies key concepts and plans that communities and governments can make to provide residences and services that create age-friendly neighborhoods.

Along with the design concepts for aging in place are the more well-known and highly regarded design fundamentals of Universal Design, many of which have been brought into the age in place realm. Universal Design is a process that uses principals that are specific to products and surroundings for the widest possible use by all people under all circumstances. It encompasses the following traits:

- Use by anyone of any ability
- Flexibility to accommodate a wide range of preferences and abilities
- Its use is easy to understand
- It effectively and easily communicates all the necessary information for use
- Minimal physical effort is involved in its use
- It has appropriate size and space for use
- The design minimizes the hazards of accidental or unintended use.

Aging in place design varies little from Universal Design, except that the intended user of age in place-friendly design elements is a defined group of older adults. Indeed, it could be difficult to distinguish one from the other, except that age in place details intentionally take into consideration the aging body's changes in vision, hearing, mobility, cognizance, balance, and a whole host of other physiological changes that occur with the natural process of the aging human body.

Indeed, this lifestyle-oriented design deals only with the structure itself. The true ability to age in place also must incorporate a myriad of other, just as important, considerations such as transportation, access to health care, and safe neighborhoods. Secondary to this is the concept that if residences incorporate these elements into new construction, we would not have to move elsewhere to retain their independence, mobility, and safety.

Although our health may be excellent at the moment, it is possible that we will experience conditions such as arthritis, possible heart or blood pressure conditions, diminished vision and hearing, or experience loss or changes in mobility.

The recommended design changes that aging in place incorporates address these issues head on. Future serious health conditions or ones that are already being monitored may require in-home health care and if this care is not available in the community where a person resides, then planning to age in that home can be compromised. Many would refer to this as a "risk assessment" or weighing the options as "pros" and "cons" regarding the probability of problems "down the road."

Second, if the cost to remodel is beyond a person's budget, then the choice to remain in the home again is not wise. A reputable contractor, remodeler, or any professional who is making design suggestions should offer choices that will fit within a person's financial circumstances, whatever they may be. In a similar vein, it may be less expensive to purchase another, more suitable home that has the home modifications and assistive technology that you need, rather than undertake remodeling or upgrading expenses. Concurrent to this is how to pay for or finance such decisions. Although reverse mortgages and Veteran's Administration financial assistance exist, not every person qualifies.

On a social level, isolation can become a serious issue when one chooses to remain in their home as he/she ages. For example, transportation to doctors, pharmacies, grocery stores, and social events, visiting family or friends, or attending religious and other activities can be stymied if one loses the ability to drive or has no one to transport them. Although many municipalities have recognized this and are making efforts to address the issue as the senior population increases, not all cities and towns have done this. Becoming isolated brings with it depression, insomnia, and a whole host of other issues. This is where senior independent and assisted living facilities can be a more appropriate choice.

Further considerations are things such as the condition of the neighborhood where the home is located. Is it safe or changing? Are the sidewalks and streets wide enough and not a hazard to walking or driving? Is the area lit well at night? What about maintenance to the home? Who will do it if we can't and how much will it cost?

As you can tell, aging in place is more than installing a grab bar! It involves a whole litany of scenarios and situations. Each of us must weigh the options available to us at that point in time to determine if remaining at home, in our own home, is the choice that is right for us.

You will find in this book a wide variety of well-thought out and demonstrated concepts that are purposely intended for the older adult, whether Baby Boomer or advanced-age senior.

A Certified Aging in Place Specialist (CAPS), Dr. Jill M. Bjerke created *Aging in Place with Grace* as a source of information and services for those who need support in determining if staying in their own home as they age is the right decision for them. She is a health care physician, international author, and sought-after speaker. She was recently appointed to the State of Iowa Commission on Aging.

References

"Americans with Disabilities Act of 1990, as Amended." *http://www.ada.gov/pubs/ada.htm*

10 Questions for . . . Michael Thomas, "Aging in Place" Expert. Nov. 4, 2008 9:49 AM. *http://news.consumerreports.org/home/2008/11/aging-in-place.html*

"The Maturing of America: Getting Communities on Track for an Aging Population." *http://www.n4a.org/pdf/MOAFinalReport.pdf*

"Partners for Livable Communities: Aging in Place Initiative." *http://livable.org/program-areas/livable-communities-for-all-ages-a-aging-in-place/programs*

"Partners for Livable Communities: The Maturing of America II." *http://livable.org/livability-resources/reports-a-publications/530-the-maturing-of-americacommunities-moving-forward-for-an-aging-population-*

"Universal Design." *http://www.washington.edu/doit/Brochures/Academics/instruction.html*

ACKNOWLEDGMENTS

After watching her grandmothers age and struggle with their independence, Naomi wanted to highlight beautiful design solutions that helped develop the concept of *Gracious Living* beyond the sterile environments that are associated with elderly facilities. Teaming up with E. Ashley Rooney, a successful, focused author, made the concept a reality. Together, they collaborated and pulled in the expertise of Dr. Jill Bjerke, who provided a well-worded Foreword. Naomi and Ashley would like to thank all the contributing architects and designers, as well as Barbara Purchia for her thoughtful proofreading. A special note of thanks to Ted K. Osborn, who recognized the initial vision of the project, and Jeff Snyder, editor.

INTRODUCTION

Naomi Neville

Working as an architect, every day I deal with codes and guidelines geared to create barrier-free environments. But I didn't consider this to be a design challenge until I experienced the aging of my two beloved grandmothers. In their late eighties, they both were faced with parallel choices of where to live, how to live, and how to maintain their fierce independence. Their homes were very different: one grandmother lived in a New York State farmhouse for fifty years, the other in a mobile home across the country in California, far from any family members. With planning and a conscious decision-making process, my Californian grandmother, Rose, at the age of eighty-six relocated to the East Coast, close to family, in a residential complex that had an elevator, easy-to-use kitchen, and a simple floor plan. Her surroundings were somewhat sterile, but she maintained the management of her daily life; she prized her independence. My grandmother Harriet, on the other hand, did not make any conscious choices about her home and instead simply stayed where she had lived year after year. But gradually, the farmhouse took its toll. It was large and rambling, requiring a great deal of maintenance. It had tight, twisty stairs and haphazard lighting. Its unique features were what gave it the character that we all loved, but some of those features became harder to work with as my grandmother grew older. As I watched these events unfold, I kept asking why can't the solution be a combination of their strategies? I began to focus on architecture to combine aging in place with universal senior-friendly design. What modifications can be made to **your** existing home to create a blend of physical comfort and safety while maintaining character and memories? Why can't the designs be beautiful?

Age creeps up on us. When young, aging is an abstract piece of common knowledge. We understand it to be inevitable but distant, when in reality we are aging with every breath. So we defy it and reject it. We see age in others but often not in ourselves. This rejection makes it difficult to plan for the future. When I first began to speak of modifying the home to suit the ever-changing needs of aging, many "older" people rejected the concept, denying the reality that their bodies will become more fragile, their existing environment more difficult to navigate. The rejection seemed based on the fears that eventually their control and independence would be taken away; that they would be removed from their homes "for their own good," and their freedom curtailed.

As designers, we try to understand the architectural limitations caused by an environment that suited us perfectly ten years before and to suggest solutions that maintain the personality and uniqueness of the individual's living space. The goal is to move beyond the mere solution of "barrier free" space; a code compliant space that feels institutional. Today's architecture is shaped by a multitude of codes and regulations, many of which address the needs of handicap accessibility. These codes do make spaces more user friendly for the elderly. But rarely are the needs of the elderly addressed at the residential level with more than the basic addition of an exterior ramp and handrails in the shower. The premise of *Gracious Living* is that thoughtful, accessible designs can be unique, tailored to the clients, and beautiful. With attention and planning, we can achieve the goal of living in our homes as we age. Architecture can find solutions that are not reactionary but instead incorporate design gradually just as our bodies gradually change and set the stage for future modifications that increase a home's flexibility turning it into a friendly, independent living space.

Not too long ago, it was commonly thought that seniors would eventually reach physical limitations that necessitated moving either into some type of healthcare facility or in with family, ensuring their safety and health needs were addressed. Family members worried that an older person's own home would become unmanageable and unsafe. Luckily, new attitudes are developing on aging and independence. With the rising number of aging baby boomers, more and more attention is being paid to the increasing ranks and needs of older people. The concept of "aging in place" is gaining in momentum and moving into mainstream design practice. Instead of skirting around the issue of limited physical functions, people are accepting it and dealing with it as a design challenge. And instead of seeing the solutions as sterile, hospital-like environments, designers are coming up with beautiful, thoughtful, and personal solutions.

What is aging in place? The concept is defined as one's ability to live in the home of his/her choosing for as long as he/she desires by taking advantage of home modifications and services that create a safe living environment. It's not a static choice; it's fluid and adaptable to one's personal desires and limitations. So, if walking becomes problematic, it's a space that works for a wheelchair. If eyesight is a problem, it's a living space with improved lighting that utilizes both task and ambient lighting. If food preparation becomes difficult, it's a home that has meals delivered. Aging in place means working towards the goal of a safe, manageable home of your choosing.

Initially, compliance with the Americans with Disabilities Act (ADA) of 1990, required public spaces to accommodate people with disabilities. Public bathrooms and reception areas with turning radiuses and counter heights suitable for a wheelchair, grab bars at toilets and showers for those with unsteady balance, or flooring changes to indicate information to blind people are all examples of ADA designs that have become more and more mainstream. Eventually, designers realized that these modifications added up to create a system known as Universal Design: architectural space that accommodates everyone to make everyday activities safe and easier for all people. Universal design is now progressing to the residential micro level, moving into individual's homes. Seeking solutions that work towards the goal of independent choice, more and more people are learning about architectural modifications to their homes that in the future will make their homes safer and more enjoyable, giving them the freedom to age in place.

The American Association of Retired Persons (AARP) has ongoing studies to understand older peoples' desires and needs to remain independent. Defining one's interpretation of independence is the first step in evaluating the years to come and how one wishes to enjoy them. For some, remaining independent is synonymous with remaining in their current home; for others it means moving to a location that allows them to walk to the grocery store so that they do not rely on a family member for a lift. Some wish for the security of an organized facility that provides many basic services and also creates an instant network of people of a similar age. Everyone is unique, and we expect that when you enter into the home of a friend, it will be different from your own. This uniqueness does not diminish with age; or just because one's eyesight diminishes, it does not mean that suddenly visual choice and desire will diminish.

When defining the focus of *Gracious Living*, we looked for two types of projects. The first type are renovations in which the homeowners made a conscious choice to remain in their home and architecturally modify their existing space. Once the choice of where and what situation had been made, the next steps were what designs could make their space suitable for their future. For example, perhaps they needed a renovated kitchen or an enlarged bathroom. The other type of projects we looked for were new construction using Universal Design solutions that are naturally integral to the home. In other words, the home does not need renovation because its initial design was in keeping with Universal Design. This book is a compilation of ideas and designs that reflect unique solutions that allow for personal expression while simultaneously working towards the goals of safe, accessible, friendly space. The solutions are evolutionary not reactionary, allowing people to engage in the decision-making process of adapting their home to fit their needs and create an individual space to be enjoyed for the many years after retirement.

References

Farber, Nicholas and Douglas Shinkle. "Aging in Place: A State Survey of Livability Policies and Practices." AARP Public Policy Institute. National Conference of State Legislatures, Jana Lynott, Wendy Fox-Grace, and Rodney Harrell. December 2011. *http://www.aarp.org/home-garden/livable-communities/info-11-2011/Aging-In-Place.html*

Love, Jeff. "Approaching 65: a survey of boomers turning 65 years old." AARP Research and Strategic Analysis from *Surveys and Statistics*. Washington, D.C., 2010.

In November 2011, the US Census Bureau stated that the nation's 90-and-older population reached 1.9 million in 2010. Because of increases in life expectancy at older ages, people 90 and above now comprise 4.7 percent of the older population (age 65 and older), as compared with only 2.8 percent in 1980. The elderly population will more than double between now and the year 2050, to 80 million. That means roughly one out of five adults in the U.S. will be over the age of 65.

One of the biggest challenges in the next 30 years will be how to meet the demand for quality living environments for the burgeoning population of older adults. This will require modifications to much of our existing housing stock, as well as making changes in new construction today that will accommodate the future physical needs of our elders.

In the following pages, we display some new residential construction and design intended for those who wish and plan to age in place.

THE HOUSE

Aging in place is a relatively new phenomenon in comparison to some of our homes that can be 50, 100, or even 150 years old. Older homes, often built before residential codes were put in place, have steep stairs, narrow doorways, or bathrooms only on the second floor. These environments make it difficult for older adults to stay in their homes as they age. Modifications such as enlarging doorway openings, increasing the width of circulation paths, and adding a full bath to the first floor can make a significant difference.

Room sizes and door widths should be able to accommodate walkers and wheelchairs. The living room, family room, or den are spaces that are often utilized as transition spaces; you must walk through the living room from the kitchen to get to the staircase. Because of their dual use of circulation, careful attention should be given to creating a path without tripping hazards.

Furniture placement and better illumination can also improve the usefulness of a space. Many possibilities exist, such as moveable furniture, e.g., a dining table that can open up for larger projects or be folded down if only used for eating. An armchair with wooden arms and a more upright back increases the ease of getting in and out of a chair. Stand up lamps can be strategically placed at a reading chair or table where more task lighting is needed. Their placement needs to consider the electrical cord to make sure that is does not inadvertently become a tripping hazard.

As people age, their sense of balance slowly diminishes, and they begin to hold onto objects to steady their trek across the room. In rooms such as the bathroom, we can easily install grab bars. The living room is somewhat different. Solid, well-balanced furniture can help function as a carefully orchestrated system of handholds and railings. The back of a sofa or the edge of a table can be a strategic but attractive grab bar. Unfortunately, the edge of a table is also handy, yet if it stands on spindly legs and holds great-grandma's imported glass vase, it is an accident waiting to happen. It is better to move the frailer furniture items out of the traffic pattern and create a path of sturdy, well placed chairs to help people navigate across the room.

A seating arrangement that sets up people to face one another is important. If a hearing problem has become severe, seating should allow for someone to sit at the elbow of another, allowing him or her to lean in. Watching the lips can become as important as hearing the sound. The acoustics of the room can be improved by fabric-covered furniture. Upholstered furniture will help to absorb the sound, whereas wood or glass will bounce the sound. Curtains or drapes can minimize unwanted background noise such as passing cars, creating a more acoustically friendly space.

Circulation paths and furniture layout must be resolved early on in order to ensure a proper passageway for wheelchairs and walkers. This design by S. Barzin Architect illustrates that point.

Flooring

Tripping accidents are more likely to happen when materials change. At any transition of materials, make sure that all the edges are laid flat, without any bumps. Carpets should either have their edges taped down or be installed with transition strips, which are used as seams between two materials. Be even more careful with area rugs because they will travel and move just a bit with each passing. Once a carpet is tripped over, the edge gets bent up; the next time a stumble happens, the edge gets bent up just a little bit more. Ultimately, it becomes a tripping hazard without being noticed.

The color of the floor materials is important. When changing materials but not shifting levels, try to keep the shades of color similar. That will minimize the hesitation caused by a dramatic color change that might be hard to understand. A color change is often associated with a level change such as a step.

Lighting and Electrical Outlets

Improved lighting is important as our eyesight diminishes. Many seniors, such as my depression-era grandmother, used low wattage bulbs to save on electricity. A stronger light will improve visibility. Installing lights on dimmers is a good way to control the light levels that are needed throughout the course of a day. A series of night lights plugged into the wall also illuminate a travel path from the bedroom to hall to bathroom. In dimly lit rooms, white or light colored paint can help to reflect the exterior light and help to brighten up a dark space.

The traditional location of electrical outlets low to the floor is not always sympathetic to an older person, who has to bend over to plug in the vacuum. If renovation allows, consider raising the outlets to a height between two to four feet above the floor.

Minimize electrical cords trailing on the floor or between pieces of furniture; consider installing recessed floor outlets. Though not ideal, a functional solution is to place flat rubber covers over cords to help keep them flat to the ground.

Coffee tables can make a pathway difficult or impossible to navigate. A side table or small drink table near a chair or seating area can create a clutter-free space. *Courtesy of Scott Moore Photography.*

A number of things make this living room designed by Pineapple House senior friendly. A low density carpet (less than ½ inch high pile) with a firm pad makes it easy to traverse with a walking aid or wheelchair. One of the two sofas in the room is very easy to get to. The wingback chairs have sturdy arms for push off and are next to a table that is easy to move around. Finally, the framed group of art has sentimental value and is a great conversation piece. *Courtesy of Scott Moore Photography.*

Windows

Windows are an important part of creating the ambiance within a room. Casement windows are a good solution in that they crank open and do not require as much physical strength to open as other window types. Casement windows open side to side and operate by use of a crank or lever. A lower sill height allows for a view when seated. A low curtain can be hung half way to help screen the residents while permitting them a view of the sky. Roman shades create the same effect. Rising from the bottom, they screen the resident first yet keep the sky visible.

These basic suggestions for your home will make it easier for you to stay as you age. Pineapple House designers offer several creative and beautiful aging in place solutions.

Elevator

An elevator is a great asset for a senior in a home. However, it may never be needed. To save the immediate expense, an elevator shaft can be put in place but intentionally serve another purpose, such as a closet, until it is desired. ◆

Thin floor coverings increase the comfort and acoustics of a floor without significantly hampering walking devices and wheelchairs. The wing chair has casters on its front legs so it can be rolled over to the game table. *Courtesy of Chris Little Photography.*

This room provides many open sitting options so its owners and guests can enjoy the picturesque view. The passageway is wide, and the center table has no sharp angles. The attached outdoor space is as inviting as it is accessible with a double width door and no transition threshold. *Courtesy of Scott Moore Photography.*

The wall behind this bench seat is upholstered to create a cozy niche. Full-draw drapery panels flanking the opening can close to block out the light and provide privacy. Seniors tend to have more problems navigating their food but the leather chair here is resistant to spills. It also offers a lower seat with stiff arms for support. A wooden drink table with an iron bottom is employed because it is easy to move.

This integrated wall/bench seat banquette can be a strong design solution if a room needs a focal point. *Courtesy of Chris Little Photography.*

A locking file drawer is integrated into the banquette built into this kitchen island. Instead of a heavy file cabinet, which tends to tip forward when drawers are open, this space-saving option is much safer for an aging user and can be accessed from either side. *Courtesy of Mon Amour Photography.*

There are clever ways to minimize obstructions in a home. This study shares a wall with the master suite. The homeowner often woke in the middle of the night with great ideas. He asked Pineapple House for easy access to his workplace because he did not want to stumble through a dark house trying to get to his desk. Pineapple House designers made the study bookshelf into a swinging wall. It is integrated so that visitors cannot detect it. It allows immediate access, and the level-grade floor makes the passage safe and wheelchair friendly. *Courtesy of Jennifer Lindell Photography.*

This room has a custom dining table that seats eight. It can be pulled apart and set up as two tables, which provides options for use that are well suited for someone in a wheelchair. Day to day, the table may only be used by one or two people, so its small size is more reflective of its use. It also is a smaller area to clean and maintain, but occasionally the table may turn into a project table or actually be used for formal dining. *Courtesy of Scott Moore Photography.*

A two-table setup offers multi-directional access, which is wonderful when entertaining. There are several seating options, including two sofas along the room's back wall. The upholstered wingback host and hostess chairs are sturdy, comfortable, and have strong arms that can be used when someone gets up. The wood dining chairs are very light and easy to move if the space is needed for a wheelchair. As parents become empty nesters, sharing a meal at a smaller table feels much more intimate. *Courtesy of Scott Moore Photography.*

Several tenants share this private elevator in a townhome. It responds to a personal pass code so doors open only into the selected private lobby. To bring light into this lobby, Pineapple House designers placed florescent bulbs behind a diffuser, then framed up a "window" on the wall. When the slats of its wooden shutters are slightly opened, "daylight" spills into the space and imparts the feeling of sunlight. A mirror on the opposite wall further reflects the glow. The nearby chairs offer respite if needed, while contributing to the beauty of the space. *Courtesy of Jennifer Lindell Photography.*

This elevator was added into an existing house, changing the existing space into an environment that will last for years. The formal elevator fits in well with the aesthetic context of the living room.

Diane Gordy, with husband, restaurateur Sike Sharigan, divides her time between her design practice based in Washington, DC and Palm Beach, recognized a 5,800 square foot owner-occupied duplex project in a mixed-use area in Palm Beach as a perfect synergy of opportunities. Her intended project honors Palm Beach's architectural legacy while its reduction in density mirrors Palm Beach's Town Council goals. "This mixed use location is exactly what the new Urbanists are talking about as a vision for re-inventing and revitalizing our cities," says Gordy. "We can walk to newsstands, restaurants, the golf course, the ocean, the post office, the grocery store. This is, simply put, the last home we will ever need." Gordy's planned procession from public to private space features garages that face the street and an open interior plan that unfolds to offer expansive views of the rear pools and garden spaces, with framed vistas featured throughout. *Photo©Angie Seckinger.*

Gordy defined a minimal palette of white, gray, and mahogany for the 2,800 square foot home that emphasizes extensive use of readily available natural materials: white stucco, white glazed ceramic tile roof, gray cast banding and parapets, concrete floors, and dark mahogany doors, windows, and Bermuda shutters. White addresses the heat; gray—seen here in the horizontal banding—ties the building into its environs, echoing adjacent art deco buildings; the richness of the mahogany and the Bermuda shutters, fixed to withstand 140-mile-an-hour winds, speak to the historic building tradition of the tropics. The muted pallet mitigates the dark and light contrasts that are often hard for older eyes to adjust to. *Photo©Angie Seckinger.*

Taking cues from the local neo-English Regency work of John Volk, one of the foremost early architects of Palm Beach, and "White Gables," his personal residence built in 1936 in the Bermuda style, Gordy introduced gables in the duplex roofline. "Gables are friendly and inviting, and a pitched roof is essential in tropical climates," she said. "I wanted to create a welcoming structure—all good design should feel gracious and inviting." *Photo©Angie Seckinger.*

The waterfall, which spills into a dipping pool, camouflages all street sounds while creating an accessible and restful retreat. Further integrating the house with the garden, Gordy designed an outdoor dining room. *Photo© Angie Seckinger.*

Mirrored surfaces expand the visual footprint of the elevator. Gordy wrapped the staircase around the elevator to create a tight core for vertical circulation. The handrail is ADA-compliant and extends beyond the treads and returns back on itself for grab ease. The stairs will accommodate non-slip strips in the future. *Photo©Angie Seckinger.*

In the open living area, Gordy kept the seating height minimum at 18 inches. The cowhide rug's low profile allows for seamless transition from the polished concrete floor to the rug, preventing a tripping hazard. The glass and stainless steel coffee table with the rounded edges is by Brueton. *Photo©Angie Seckinger.*

Green accents, found in the Murano sconces and the bookcase designed by Gordy, connect with the foliage outside the sliding glass doors. The consistent height of the door openings—the sliding glass doors are Maytag—and that of the bookcase establishes a regulating line around the room. *Photo©Angie Seckinger.*

Under-sink shelving in the 3-½ baths is removable to accommodate the potential need for wheelchair access. The Lacava lavatories are ADA height. The Bermuda shutters provide privacy throughout the house and eliminate the need for window treatments. In the master bath, Gordy raised the height of the custom-designed counters to allow for comfortable use. Grab bars are installed in the open shower, which features a seating area. *Photo©Angie Seckinger.*

Left and opposite page: The kitchen is designed around the 60-inch diameter turning space required for a wheelchair. The Decora cabinets feature pulls instead of knobs. The recessed track lighting, housed in trays painted the same tone as the mahogany doors, delineate and light the space. The countertops are bianco carrara marble with gray veining, a material reinforcing Gordy's color palette, which is also found in the garden fountain wall and windowsills throughout. The appliances are Viking; the oversized sink is Franke and features a Lacava faucet. *Photo©Angie Seckinger.*

The Victoria Garden Mews is a four unit condominium project consisting of two buildings—the front building, a 2,520 square foot Victorian (which replaced the original 1890s home on the lot), and the rear building, a 5,100 square foot, three unit Spanish style residential building—built utilizing the City of Santa Barbara's architectural design guidelines. The design team partnership between Thompson Naylor Architects and Allen Associates began with a question from Dennis Allen, the project visionary and general contractor: "Want to try and build the most sustainable development possible in historic downtown Santa Barbara and then move in together to form an intentional community built around food, beauty, and friendship?" *Courtesy of Jim Bartsch.*

The partners included elevators to make it possible to live comfortably in the two-story Victorian unit and the three-story condominium building in the back. The elevator in the front house has design elements that tie it into the overall Victorian aesthetic of the home, such as painted wainscoting and casings.

Because the partners were planning to live in this home for as long as possible, they made all the doorways wider than 30 inches to allow for wheelchair access if needed. They had levers installed instead of standard doorknobs, as well as an ADA accessible shower.

Aging in place is "the ability to live in one's own home and community safely, independently, and comfortably." As a result, a project's location and its community linkages are important factors to consider. This project's downtown infill location, close to public transportation and numerous community services, also add to its sustainability. *Courtesy of Meghan Beierle-O'Brien Photography.*

One goal of the partnership was to create a project that was as close to net zero energy as possible—with buildings that produced as much energy as they consumed. Green building elements in this third floor condominium unit include passive solar design, reclaimed wood floors and beams, sustainably harvested wood, LED lighting, and low Volatile Organic Compound (VOC) finishes on the kitchen cabinets. Foregoing traditional paint, American Clay Earth Plaster, a natural, environmentally friendly plaster, was used as the finish coat on the interior walls. *Courtesy of Meghan Beierle-O'Brien Photography.*

In addition to being the primary gathering place during parties, this kitchen in the Victorian building is well lit and has easily accessible storage. *Courtesy of Meghan Beierle-O'Brien Photography.*

The homeowners wanted Peter Brock, Architect, to design a new house that was compact, convenient, and capable of adapting to their family's evolving mobility—destined to be the last house they would need to own. Attention to accessibility begins at the bus stop immediately in front of the house. From there a landscaped ramp interweaves with steps to deliver visitors to the front door with equal grace, whatever their mobility. There is also a three-stop elevator to bring the owners and all manner of materials effortlessly to any floor of the house.

The main stair fans out like lava to create a bench seat that, with the window seats, ensures you're never far from a pleasant place to catch your breath. A custom made wood-capped steel "bamboo" handrail makes a firm and friendly grip for arthritic hands.

The halls and doorways are extra wide with wheelchair-friendly clearances. While the house's three floors take advantage of the sloped site and dramatic views, all of the core functions of the owners' lives—living, dining, kitchen, laundry, master bedroom and bath—are housed on the main floor. Super-insulated walls and ceilings, photovoltaic panels, and under floor radiant heating ensure quiet, dust free, uniform, economical comfort. Programmable lighting and heating make the physical environment easy to control while low maintenance finishes and central vacuum keep it easy to clean.

A large opening between the kitchen and living room allows the two modestly scaled rooms to borrow each other's spatial extent and physically join together in accommodating large gatherings. The strong wooden arms of the sofa help with getting in and out of the seats. The large bank of windows provides ample natural light.

The kitchen is laid out around a central table rather than an island so that it can be moved to accommodate multiple work surface heights and changing needs for clearance. The oven arrangement is convenient, the stove is configured for wheelchair knee space, dishes are stowed low, and the dishwasher is held high to minimize both reaching and stooping.

Even on the second floor, family and friends with limited mobility can enjoy the outdoors by means of a hallway window seat or bedroom balcony.

Both the master bath and guest bath include wheelchair-friendly, curb-less shower stalls with fold-down seats. Extra turning room and knee space under the counters ensure ease of access. Bright task lighting at the mirrors helps older eyes see.

The rhythm of entry pilasters and ceiling coffers offers a sense of movement as one passes through the flush entry threshold in this penthouse owned by an active retired couple. The enhanced color saturation of the floor, table, and art frame increases their definition. The interior designers at Deep River Partners employed muted wall and trim colors to become the museum-like backdrop for the valued art collection. *Courtesy of Mark F. Heffron.*

An open and airy floor plan boasts panoramic views of Lake Michigan and beyond. The transitional style imparted by the designers at Deep River calls on traditional roots while promoting a clean line that unites the contemporary high rise exterior with a more welcoming, livable, and traditional interior. Properly scaled furniture creates generous circulation paths, and the flexibility in furniture arrangements is unencumbered. The rhythm of wall sconces and paneled cased openings define the perimeter and form a separation from the contemporary curtain wall beyond. *Courtesy of Mark F. Heffron.*

Condominium living reduces exterior maintenance requirements and provides for everyday concierge amenities. In this project, the design team at Deep River Partners blended art, architecture, and interiors into a seamless whole that promotes the comfortable gathering of family and friends. While the grand stair is prominent in the foyer, an in-suite elevator is also available to access the second floor library. Note the creative design on the handrail. *Courtesy of Mark F. Heffron.*

The comfortable seating area in the bedroom suite is convenient for visiting and makes available a nearby upright seating option. The automated drop down TV is neatly concealed in the ceiling when not in use. Self-illuminated push button keypads conveniently located at the bedside control lighting, window shades, and temperature, allowing for an infinite spectrum of comfortable atmosphere options. *Courtesy of Joe DeMaio Photography.*

Richly stained walnut casework warms the library, which doubles as a guest room, complete with a hidden Murphy bed behind the paneling. Abundant shelving houses a lifelong legacy of favorite books and artifacts from world travels. The hidden large screen is readily available if desired, and larger horizontal pulls ease cabinet access. Defining one's life experiences and prompting stimulation through reading, writing, and watching all bring about an enriched daily life. *Courtesy of Joe DeMaio Photography.*

Going down. Hopefully not! This 60+-year-old couple has been living in their home for the last thirty years, and every one of those years has been spent climbing up and down this steep bulkhead to get to the washer and dryer. *Courtesy of Nat Rea.*

Technically, they had a garage, but the family automobile didn't fit in it. This area was used for storage. The garage and breezeway were wasted spaces. *Courtesy of Nat Rea.*

They contacted Brusco Design & Renovation to give them more living space for their extended family and a new laundry area on the first floor. Doorways were made as wide as possible to accommodate wheelchair or walker traffic later in life. *Courtesy of Nat Rea.*

The completed family room is insulated 50 percent better than local building code requirements and has triple-glazed windows to reduce drafts and noise. A gas fireplace provides added warmth and ambiance. The laundry area is now accessible, and a large closet behind the TV/fireplace wall provides their storage space. *Courtesy of Nat Rea.*

The living room is now the dining room. The opening between the kitchen and front room was expanded to 10 feet. Not only did this make the home feel larger, it made wheelchair and walker traffic possible in the future. Door levers replaced doorknobs throughout the house for ease of use. *Courtesy of Nat Rea.*

The North Fork Residence exemplifies what Thielsen Architects refers to as a "Two Story Rambler." Thielsen uses this term to describe a house where all spaces and functions used by the clients on a daily basis are located on the main floor. There are no steps or changes in floor elevation anywhere on the main level, including the transition from the garage into the house or from the house to the many exterior terraces and decks. All of the spaces are accessed through 36-inch wide doors and generously sized hallways to accommodate future wheelchair use.

The upper floor of the home is nestled into the hillside, but glazed on three sides, producing an exciting space which feels intimately connected to the landscape. The simple yet striking shed roof form echoes the slopes of the surrounding mountains. Currently, the secondary spaces on the upper level are accessed by an elegant straight-run stair, but allowance has been made for the installation of an elevator should it be desired in the future. The owners, one of whom is an octogenarian, presently enjoy travelling up and down the stair as a form of gentle exercise.

The exterior courtyard is fully accessible from the interior and provides both built-in seating and space for flexible furniture arrangements. Windows facing the court provide inviting views of the outdoor living space and the mountains surrounding the home on all sides. The exterior palette of metal and stone was selected specifically because it requires very little maintenance, even in the harsh weather conditions common in the home's mountainous setting. The low maintenance landscaping features many native plants, which require less water and care than most ornamental hybrids.

Extensive built-in storage is provided throughout the home, which allows flexible furniture arrangements. This means that as access needs change, the furniture can be adjusted to provide additional room for circulation without compromising the functionality of the spaces. The large windows throughout the home provide bright and balanced natural light, which results in plentiful illumination and very little glare.

Generous circulation space in the master bedroom is combined with extensive built-in cabinets to yield a clean and serene composition. The high-quality recessed light fixtures used in the master suite, and throughout the home, produce a warm and even light with virtually no glare. Facing east and north to invite in the morning sun, the large windows feature inspiring views of valley and mountains beyond and open for pleasant natural ventilation. In the master bathroom, the vanities were designed to allow wheelchair access; the master shower has a roll-in floor, and grab bars have already been installed.

The built-in cabinets and display spaces of the central circulation spine create a sense of place, which invites the occupants to stop and enjoy the experience, making it more of a room than just a hallway. With windows along its length and glazed doors at both ends, this gallery is an inviting and pleasant space through which the owners enjoy traveling. The generous width means that a person in a walker or wheelchair could travel side by side with an ambulatory individual. The stair has handrails on both sides.

The dining room features ample circulation space and open access to the kitchen and gallery. The porcelain tile floor is currently softened by area rugs, which can be easily removed to yield a smooth hard floor easy for walking and, if need be, wheelchairs. The kitchen features wider than typical working floor space allowing circulations behind the cook and easy navigation in a walker or wheelchair.

This Colorado Mountain home had been pre-designed without consideration for mobility issues for a 92-year-old woman and an empty nester couple with crippling arthritis and diminishing vision. Sandra Elizabeth Clinger, the designer, together with the homeowners, worked to provide wheelchair access and accommodations for present and anticipated future limitations. The result is that the home supports the homeowners' physical, emotional, and aesthetic needs. The no-step entry leads onto level surfaces from one flooring material to another, including hardwood with acrylic-impregnated surface in a non-skid finish. Carpet was installed to reduce sound transmission. The transom windows above doors enable natural cross lighting. Hallways and bathrooms are framed and pre-blocked for future support bars should they be needed. The hallways and doorways are built wide enough to accommodate a wheelchair.

The furniture is designed for comfortable wheelchair roll-up. Window heights are lowered to provide a captivating view of the Colorado Mountains from chair or bed. A staircase between floors is designed to accommodate a chairlift.

Soft, rounded corners and rounded countertop edges avoid bruising.

The kitchen features room for a wheelchair and cross lighting for the owners who need strong light. The microwave is installed at countertop level so those with arthritis do not have to reach. The counter in front of the microwave enables the user to set things down quickly. The dishwasher height is 42 inches. The breakfast bar is 30 inches high, which is a comfortable height to roll up to in a wheelchair or to use with a standard stool or chair. Multiple sources of light balance natural light and make it easy on the eye.

The bathroom avoids the need for an area rug by using a built-in carpet of tile with slip resistant sanded grout. The contrasting countertop edge treatment aids in finding the edge easily. Glare is avoided through finish material selection and location of fixtures.

A no-threshold, door-less shower enables ease of ambulation. The shower has a bench and handheld shower attachment. The toilet has an 18 inch seat height.

Levers and wrist blades are appealing to users with impaired function.

The spacious home designed by Rebecca Soechtig of RED Interior looks much like any "normal" home, while being equipped for the future. A firm sofa allows the residents to get out of the sofa more easily than a soft one. Wooden floors are a clean and functional choice. They are warm and inviting when accented with throw rugs that can easily be removed for a walker or wheelchair. Pretty French doors are a clever way to provide access to the outdoors by simply adding a small ramp if necessary.

The beautiful powder room sports a toilet/bidet combo, heated seat, and a remote to take care of sanitary needs, great for people who have difficulty getting in and out of the shower or tub daily. The vessel sink is a focal point, and its elegant lever handle faucet allows for easy control of pressure and temperature.

The overhang on the island creates a seated work area. Well-placed undercounter outlets allow for safe hand-held appliance usage. The built-in refrigerator is cleverly placed so as not to reduce the width of the aisles.

The chef who owns this house insisted upon a gas cook top. This cook top has the controls located on the front for use in a seated position if necessary. Controls located in this position also eliminate the need to reach past the burners to turn the knobs. The unique copper counter provides beauty on a surface that kills bacteria and microbes on contact. The paver tile floor provides a rustic, old world look but is slip-resistant thanks to the cunning use of the wider crossing grout lines. The aisle widths are 44–48 inches, designed so drawers can stay open and people can still pass through with ease.

The oven is raised slightly off the floor for easier access, and the microwave is set slightly above counter height for easy use. The storage cabinets on the front of the island are only 12 inches deep for formal china and silver used in the nearby dining room.

Two 25-inch deep pantries have roll-out shelves to access groceries handily.

These contemporary cabinets are as smart as they appear: all drawers have been designed for easy access and use. The pull out style eliminates the need to awkwardly reach into the back of the cabinets. You don't have to get on the floor to reach into the back of a cabinet. They are easy to keep clean, and the long, stainless handles allow grips at variable heights based on the homeowners' evolving needs.

The current master bedroom can easily be converted to a guest room, should the owners need to move downstairs because of mobility issues. A main level guest bedroom can be converted to a first floor master.

The current master bath has a no-slip floor. Shallow vessel sinks provide the convenience of a normal sink while single lever faucets can be used by anyone with ease.

The downstairs bathroom has cabinet doors below the sinks, which can be removed for roll-up wheelchair access. The stylish Mexican tiles with their fleur-de-lis pattern provide low-slip flooring.

This Landmarks designated site was built prior to World War II. The interior architecture has the typical "pre-war" details, such as wide hallways, ample doorways, and tall ceilings. The apartment is accessible via an elevator from the building lobby. Hilary Unger of Perianth Interior Design/Buy My Eye® found plenty of room for wheelchair access and turn-around space in the entry, as well as to the apartment from the elevator just outside the door. The ebonized chest provides a convenient place for warm weather accessories as well as a place for mail and keys. The entry way is well lit, with light switches placed conveniently throughout the apartment at the New York City code height. *Photo by Michael Falco.*

The single-story apartment has no steps between the main rooms, bedrooms, and corridors. The large rooms of the apartment allow for easy flow around the furniture, especially in the dining room. The six-arm chandelier, along with the console table lamp, provides ample light for the dining room and, during the day, there is a nice amount of natural daylight through the windows. The windows open easily because they have a bottom horizontal lip. *Photo by Michael Falco.*

In the master bedroom, different levels of lighting are provided, including ceiling, wall, and task for overall illumination. Windows on two sides of the room provide cross breeze ventilation as well as abundant natural light. The mirror reflects the light further. There is plenty of room for movement around the bed. The area rug is a low density carpet with a firm pad. In addition, the contrast from dark wood floor to light carpet indicates a change in surface levels, which is helpful for maneuvering around the space. The illuminated closets have adjustable closet rods allowing for flexibility in use. The pull handles on the dresser provide for easy access to the drawers. *Photo by Michael Falco.*

The main middle bath is large enough to be classified as an ADA bathroom with a 5-foot wheelchair turn-around. The bath utilizes cross handles for the faucet and tub fittings, and the tub/shower controls are offset from the center. There is a flush-mounted ceiling light fixture, as well as a three-arm wall sconce over the mirror, illuminating the entire bathroom. The toilet seat can be switched out to be height adjustable. *Photo by Michael Falco.*

The existing single story house made a good start to an aging in place home. Previous expansions created a collection of rooms strung together by long, dark corridors making it cumbersome to get around. The remodel by architects Peter Brock and Marina Rubina eliminated long, narrow halls where one had to struggle to find a light switch in the dark. The new addition combined the narrow circulation spaces and a deck into a light-filled family room whose direct connection to the surrounding rooms brings unprecedented unity and ease of access. *Courtesy of Tomasz Klys.*

The formerly dark and dead-ended kitchen now flows and opens to the rooms around it. Having two ways in and out eliminates the need for a turning radius, allowing the kitchen to remain compact. All appliances are close together so that one can merely turn from one to the other without having to walk far. Most contents are brought within reach via a built-in pantry and extensive lower drawers. *Courtesy of Tomasz Klys.*

The merger of large-scale gathering and small-scale nooks and workstations in the family room allows one space to serve multiple modes for each family member simultaneously. One can spend all day in the same room, but have a place for a variety of activities. The computer and writing desk with adjacent built-in filing cabinets keep papers within reach and organized. A bench near the window serves as a reading nook, a place to enjoy the view of the yard, or a resting spot for putting on shoes on the way to the garden. A French door rather than a sliding door eliminates a tripping hazard of a bottom track. *Courtesy of Tomasz Klys.*

Numerous new sources of natural light give life to rooms once dark and compartmentalized. The family room skylight is motorized, providing natural ventilation at a push of a button, reducing or completely eliminating the need for supplemental air conditioning. This new family room and kitchen remodel simplified the layout of the house, improved access, created gathering and private spaces, and added natural light and ventilation, thus extending the house's viability as a functional and attractive vessel for an evolving family. *Courtesy of Tomasz Klys.*

This classic mid-century home is typically a single story with simple straight lines and without level changes or obstacles. This same theme translates throughout the house, easily accommodating most age-related mobility concerns. The client asked Brion Jeannette Architecture to add the living amenities appropriate for 2012 without sacrificing the integrity of the 1960s design style. *Courtesy of Marcie Heitzmann.*

Mid-century modern homes embrace an open floor plan, much like the classic "Great Room" design concept popular today. Walls are minimal, allowing for wide circulation and easy access from one room to the next; wheelchairs and walkers can move unrestricted. Light and ventilation are important elements that make all of our lives feel good, at any age. But, plenty of bright, natural light is essential to help an aging population function easily as eyesight can be diminished with advancing years. Dual pane glass was installed for energy efficiency and to help the home maintain a more constant temperature. *Courtesy of Marcie Heitzmann.*

Interestingly, this home's style and layout proves to be multi-generational—appealing not only to a family with young children, but easily accommodating an older generation whose living requirements focus around accessibility and convenience. Because of the openness of the mid-century floor plan, interaction for activities from one room to the next, and from inside to outside, is seamless. *Courtesy of Marcie Heitzmann.*

Minor modifications were made to this master suite that makes it particularly comfortable for seniors aging in place. The typical door was eliminated and replaced with a decorative, wide sliding door, enhancing access between the bedroom and bathroom. A sliding door was added to provide additional light and ventilation and direct access to the backyard. The rear yard was designed with artificial turf that eliminates constant maintenance and looks great year round—especially ideal for an aging resident. *Courtesy of Marcie Heitzmann.*

Everything in this kitchen is within easy reach. There are no physical obstacles to navigate, and its openness allows constant interaction with others in the family room or dining room. The laundry room is conveniently located directly off the kitchen. *Courtesy of Marcie Heitzmann.*

The clients wanted a house for their future. Deep River Partners took great care in the details that provide ease of use at every step. Automated glass walls open to reveal the awesome natural setting beyond and draw one to the outdoors. The semitransparent sunshade reduces glare and heat gain at the touch of a button. A concealed track in the floor is seamless and flush. The large table without legs at the perimeter allows for unencumbered seating. The gentle waterfall fills the air with tranquility in the desert quiet. © *Erhard Pfeiffer 2012.*

The open plan flows between rooms while varying the ceiling heights and inserting textural volumes such as the glass mosaic tile at the fire feature creates special definition. Richard Sherer, design principal at Deep River Partners, utilizes concealed toe-kick lighting to provide brightness at the perimeter, marking the cabinet edges. With focused, small aperture down lights that have minimal glare, maximum task brightness is maintained at the counter surfaces while the overall mood remains subdued. Refrigerator drawers concealed in the foreground cabinets are easy to reach, and single lever, hands free faucets function without effort. © *Erhard Pfeiffer 2012.*

The guest suite provides increased independence at the main residence. The Deep River team of architects and interior designers designed the guest suite to be self-contained with its own living, sleeping, dining, and cooking spaces. Adjacent to the main residence and connected via an outdoor courtyard, the separate living quarters allow for interaction with the main residence yet protect privacy and allow for the separation of generations if desired. The main level master bedroom and accessible bath accommodate all age groups. © *Erhard Pfeiffer 2012.*

An aspect of universal design in residential architecture can be defined as providing environments where all age groups can flourish. The interior and exterior space blend to create an environment that allows for many different activities and a broad range of user groups. The whirlpool is outfitted with many seating heights and connects to the main pool via a water slide for the more adventurous. The beach edge offers effortless access to ease into the water and gives an even shallower end for the youngest. The linear dimension of the pool supports lap swimming while cascading steps double as refreshing lounge seating. The elevated terrace level affords a jumping area into the deep water below. Ready for recreation and relaxation, this water feature transforms to support every desire and ability. © *Erhard Pfeiffer 2012.*

THE KITCHEN

Kitchen planning is extremely personal, and there are numerous kitchen layout designs to choose from. In an age-friendly kitchen, the goal is to increase the flexibility of the space, preparing for the unknown and creating an environment that creates useful options for how to use and function in the space. When planned to incorporate any physical changes over time, these kitchens will end up beautiful and enjoyable spaces.

When designing an age-friendly kitchen, the builder needs to consider any physical constraints that may already or will be present (e.g., ease of access) and the existing space, such as, the location of windows, the width and depth of the room, and the location of plumbing and wiring. Before starting to plan the kitchen, take time to think about how it is used. Is it a place hidden from guests? A food preparation space only; or does it double as a place to greet and entertain guests? Is it the main family gathering place, and, if so, how many cooks will be in the kitchen? When the different roles of the kitchen are defined, then the spatial needs will become clear. The homeowner's decision-making process will help define the needs for lighting, floor materials, counter heights, and cabinets. Then consider common aging issues such as trouble with hearing, movement, and the possibility of needing a wheelchair—will it still be useful? You can't foresee everything, but do consider the future.

The traditional work triangle of sink, range, and refrigerator is a well-tested arrangement. The classic arrangement uses an L-shaped counter or a kitchen island counter, and the appliances are approximately 36 to 48 inches away from one another. In between each appliance is free counter space. But other basic kitchen layouts, such as the U-shape, galley, and one-wall plans, can be used when planning a universal aging in place kitchen.

A simple layout provides easy access to and from the sink, stove, and refrigerator. Each appliance should have adjacent counter space and an unobstructed floor space in front of each appliance, preferably 48 x 30 inches. Layout options depend on the available space. If space is tight, it's better to utilize a simple plan rather than cramming a lot into a compact, congested space.

The traditional counter height of 36 inches continues to be a useful counter height for most people while standing. This height feels comfortable and does not necessitate leaning over. For an older person, however, this height can feel too high when it is necessary to chop vegetables or stir a cake mix because it is harder to use your body weight as leverage. To increase the kitchen's flexibility, one counter area should be built at a lower height (i.e., between 28 and 32 inches), which allows a person to work while seated. The 30 inch counter height is useful for people who find standing to be more difficult, need the additional leverage of the weight of their body, or are confined to a wheelchair. Remember to keep the space underneath the lower counter clear of obstructions.

Each major appliance should be adjacent to a counter. This counter space can be used for placing objects, such as a hot baking dish from the oven or a heavy pot in the refrigerator. Two appliances can share the same counter space.

Cabinets

The most useful cabinets are lower base cabinet storage and full height storage cabinets. Pull-out drawers, with full extension drawer slides, will dramatically increase the accessibility of the contents of below the counter cabinets. Pulling the cabinet's contents out eliminates the need to bend down and peer into the recesses of a deep cabinet. Specialty drawers are becoming more readily available and offer a great flexibility about the height of their installation. Warming drawers and freezer/refrigerator drawers are options for versatile appliance placement.

Building a variety of counter heights can increase a kitchen's future adaptability. The kitchen shown has the main counter at 36 inches but one segment is built at 30 inches. Currently, the owners use the lower counter as a desk but in the future, this counter area would also be useful as a preparation area if the cook needed to sit down while working or needed a lower surface while chopping vegetables. The lower counter allows for a person's body weight to push on the knife, augmenting an older person's strength.

Naomi Neville designed a kitchen renovation, built by Patrick's Residential Property Management, to incorporate a variety of aging in place concepts. Compact in plan, the majority of the storage is in a full height cabinet, maximizing the shoulder to waist accessible storage space; the island has two counter heights and the sink has a levered faucet. The microwave is built into the island just under the counter to eliminate the need to reach up to the microwave.

By paneling the ceiling, there is no stark glare often caused by an over bright white ceiling. Recessed down lights are used in conjunction with decorative task pendants and matching blinds, giving the homeowners ultimate control over the ambience of the light.

Another nice aspect of this kitchen renovation project is that the side-by-side refrigerator was original. By refacing it with a new cabinet face, there was no need to buy a new appliance.

Upper cabinets become less useful and more dangerous as the homeowner ages. All those delicate bowls stacked up on the second shelf get difficult to get down. The lowest row is useful from a standing height. The second and third shelf though become problematic and may require a step stool. A sturdy step stool can help extend the use of high shelving, but is not always recommended for the aging homeowner. Guardrails across the shelves might be a good idea if glass is stored higher up, so that a shaky hand doesn't pull down more than the expected glass.

The best storage is a full height cabinet with storage in the doors as well. The homeowner can walk straight up to its contents. All kitchens should have at least one full-length storage cabinet in a convenient spot. There also should be storage at waist to chest height for all those plates, glasses, and bowls.

The Sink

A good height for a person standing at a sink is approximately 36 inches with a bowl depth of 7 inches. A deeper bowl may lead to stooping. If room allows, a two-bowl sink, one deep, one shallow, is the best of both worlds. Add a garbage disposal and a side drying rack, and one has a nice dishwashing station. Sinks that are mounted underneath the counter are easier to clean because they do not have a protruding lip edge. Using an undermount sink also allows for more flexible placement of the faucet; mounting the faucet to the side of the sink brings the faucet closer to the user and helps with access.

The faucet itself should be a lever handle that can be pushed or pulled from side to side, eliminating the need to twist or turn a knob. Installing a spray nozzle on your kitchen sink will add a lot of flexibility to cleaning and food preparation and can either be integral to the main sink faucet or installed as a separate smaller faucet.

Appliances

As age takes a toll on eyesight, seeing the temperature on the small dials across the counter becomes increasingly difficult. Avoid using stoves with the knobs on the rear of the appliance as it requires reaching across the burners to turn them on or off and this action creates a situation in which someone might get burned or accidentally start a fire. When choosing between a gas and electric stove, consider whether you want the easy-to-see gas flames or the convenience of a flat electric range top. Often when an electric stove is turned off, the appearance of the burners returns to normal before the temperature does. Because of diminished circulation, an older person does not feel the temperature as quickly as a younger person if he/she accidentally touches a burner. Induction cooktops have become a popular third alternative for stoves, as they work by making a pot or pan generate its own heat electromagnetically; therefore, induction cooktops do not transfer heat. When the pot or pan is removed from the surface, the stove cools down within seconds, eliminating the possibility of burning the user.

A built-in oven mounted at counter height can mitigate the need to lift food up or down into the oven. Control panels should be simple and clear, with large illuminated numbers and large knobs for easy on and off. An interior light and self-cleaning features increase the age-friendly quality of the oven.

A side-by-side refrigerator provides easy access storage for both the refrigerator and freezer. Both sides have equal accessibility with a convenient central portion and waist height access. Some people prefer the freezer on the bottom so they can look down into the contents, but they are still forced to lean down to pick something up. The high freezers have a similar problem in that you have to reach up for something, and often it is difficult to see up and towards the back. Pull-out drawers help with storage organization.

The primary sink faucet, filtered water spigot, and adjustable pot filler in this kitchen designed by Pineapple House all employ single levers that integrate the fixture's temperature control and water flow. The knobs on the stove are large, easy to read, and conveniently located. *Courtesy of Scott Moore Photography.*

Ideally, microwaves would be mounted at a lower height than what we typically find above a stove. Today, microwaves can be found mounted in a base cabinet, on the counter, or built into a full height cabinet. If a homeowner is in a wheelchair, the counter space under the microwave should be clear.

Raising a dishwasher 9 to 12 inches off the floor decreases the distance one bends over and is another way to make an appliance easier to use.

Kitchen Lighting

Natural light in the kitchen will increase the usability and friendliness of the space.

There are three main lighting strategies for kitchen lighting:

- Create a uniform, even spread of light. An array of recessed LED lights casts a uniform glow. When put on a dimmer, the lights can be adjusted for time of day and outside ambient light.
- Accent main spaces with decorative task lighting. For example, a series of pendant lights hung over an island can help with food preparation and improve the appearance of the kitchen.
- Highlight workspaces with functional recessed or undercounter lighting. Additional lighting at work areas, especially at perimeter counters, can increase the overall usability of the kitchen by directing a stronger source of light onto a smaller surface area.

The combination of these lighting strategies creates an environment that is comfortable for the eyes of both the guest and user. To add even more flexibility and adjustability, place all the lights on dimmers and separate switches. Light switches should be placed at entries and exits from the space and at work areas where additional task lighting might be needed.

Details and Amenities

The colors of the cabinets and counters should be selected based on the specific eyesight characteristics of the homeowner. Everyone's eyesight changes as they age, and different conditions can develop, changing the way people see colors. In some cases, choosing contrasting colors will help to distinguish one object from another, such as choosing a dark counter surface next to a light colored cabinet. Other people may need to avoid choosing too light of a color because it tends to accentuate glare.

Keeping the kitchen clean is an important aspect of maintaining the homeowner's independence, so choosing a durable, smooth countertop finish is important. Easy to clean counter surfaces such as granite or solid surface materials can simplify tasks in the kitchen.

Convenient Ground Fault Circuit Interrupter (GFCI) waterproof electrical outlets at counter level increase the flexibility of using small kitchen appliances. Mounting outlets directly onto the edge of an island counter's edge eliminates the need to stretch appliance cords, which can be a safety hazard. Convenient outlets also increase the flexibility of the island's use, allowing it to temporarily serve other purposes.

Adding a pass-through window between the kitchen and other spaces, such as a dining room or living room, can decrease travel time and distance for carrying in food. If you can, add a counter on either side of the window, flush to the opening so that items can be gently pushed and pulled from one side to another.

Kitchens are often entered through a back entry such as a mudroom or garage. Adding a bench or counter near the back entry adds a convenient spot to rest or put down groceries. A dumbwaiter is another construction amenity that can be very convenient depending on the layout. It can bring groceries from a lower garage to an upper kitchen or laundry from an upper bedroom down to a wash room.

This Pineapple House kitchen has a pasta pot filler, a range and ovens with front controls, an integrated prep sink in the island, and electrical outlets that are placed high on the base of the island for easy access. *Courtesy of Jennifer Lindell Photography.*

Pineapple House designers recommend using pull-out drawers that allow access to items in the rear sections whenever possible. *Courtesy of Rob Downey Photography.*

Carolyn Cook of LiveSmart Design did an interior remodel for an older healthy adult who wished to have her wheelchair-bound granddaughter visit overnight. The kitchen is designed to be beautiful, flexible, and adaptable. The small mobile island with open shelving allows the homeowner to relocate the island in the event of mobility impairment and provides open visibility to the space. Most people of varied age and ability can easily access drawers located below counter height, including the double drawer dishwasher, the bottom drawer freezer, and the base-cabinet drawers. The room has balanced lighting to assist with visual impairment that may occur with age. It combines natural light, task lighting, and ambient lighting. A wall-hung lighted glass-front cabinet allows visibility at a glance without opening doors. Good contrast is provided between the floor and cabinets, and non-glare finishes are in place. Acoustics are improved by the use of a quiet over-the-range hood removing harmful cooking toxins from the home.

The table and chairs were the first purchase made by the homeowner and her husband. The combination of "old and new" makes the space both intimate and personable. To allow complete mobility, the door leading into the kitchen was widened, making the entire home accessible to her young granddaughter's wheelchair. The small mobile island and lightweight chairs can be moved easily to allow for maximum access. The lack of area rugs on the wooden floor promotes maneuverability and safety, while the wooden floor provides acoustical value.

This microwave drawer is perfect for all ages and abilities. Most homes have the microwave above the cook top, and we never give it a thought. But if you hurt your back or are temporarily disabled, you can't safely reach the microwave with pots cooking below. The addition of pullout drawers and work surface above makes this location an ideal secondary cook station.

Aging in place designers such as Pineapple House consider what people need to stay in control of their environment and, thereby, continue living at home. Good nutrition is critical to a healthy lifestyle. The kitchen needs to be especially user-friendly so an elderly person can efficiently prepare their meals. *Courtesy of Scott Moore Photography.*

RED Interior created a kitchen that features hidden outlets under a counter-height bar, a key to autonomy, allowing users to cook and use hand-held appliances at a seated working surface. The convenient outlets also mitigate the long appliance cords that often cause accidents for all ages. Interior designer Rebecca Soechtig points out that "there's nothing like wooden floors for both beauty and a soft feel underfoot. Softer flooring choices are especially important to those who are challenged with footing or balance issues."

Pull-out pantries are a brilliant way to provide for easy access to daily foods or dishware at lower heights.

This induction cook top is a safe surface that uses magnetic heat, leaving the cooking area touchable seconds after removing the cooking vessel. A four-light hood provides maximum light for cooking. The 3-foot wide door openings allow better access for walkers and wheelchairs, or an arm full of groceries.

This drawer microwave is sleek and functional. Located below the counter, this drawer is a super asset for those challenged by lifting, bending, or utilizing their upper body. It is also easily accessible by wheelchairs and visiting grandchildren.

WINNER OF THE 2008 NATIONAL HOME BUILDER'S ASSOCIATION "HOME FOR LIFE" AWARD FOR KITCHENS

The client was left at a 4-foot 6-inch height as a result of surgery. Her priorities when she went to Leslie Shankman-Cohen of Jill Hertz Interior Design were an open kitchen that made her happy, easy access to all utensils, and better lighting. She also did not want the kitchen to look or feel like it was in any way modified for a smaller person. The result is a much larger and open area, which allows for future wheelchair accessibility throughout.

Leslie Shankman-Cohen incorporated and featured the original tile from the hall into a softer bamboo floor, a sustainable and renewable product. To accommodate any future issues, accessible 9-inch toe kicks were used throughout. In addition, custom-designed step platforms were installed under the stove and sink areas, eliminating the need to move a step stool around for access. The homeowner can easily access these platforms by pulling them out with her feet—no bending! They are on rollers with a kickstand lock on the side, rendering them very stable. In addition, they hold in excess of 300 pounds in weight. If, in the future, they become unnecessary because of wheelchair accessibility issues, they are completely removable.

WINNER OF THE 2008
NATIONAL HOME BUILDER'S ASSOCIATION
"HOME FOR LIFE" AWARD FOR KITCHENS

Upper cabinets next to the stove were fitted with interior shelving units that easily pull "out and down" to counter height for easy access. Deep drawers were installed in lower cabinets to accommodate heavy pots and pans. Additionally, dishes were located in custom dish holders in the lower cabinets next to the sink for ease of access. The pantry and all other lower cabinets were fitted with roll-out shelving, allowing for easy access.

An appliance garage, adjacent to the baking area, was fitted with electrical strip outlets for easy access to appliances without the need to move or lift them to another prep area. A recycling center was set up under the cabinet, as well as a kitchen composting bin under the vegetable prep area.

Custom designed birch veneer cabinets were installed as well as quartz countertops. Custom, handmade tiles were used to create the backsplash design. Glass tiles with metal insets were used on the under cabinet backsplash. Because continuous counter space was at a premium, adjustable counter heights were not an option. Therefore, all the counters were lowered from the standard 36 inch to a 34 inch height, an almost imperceptible difference. This allowed the upper cabinets to be proportionately lowered by 2 inches.

WINNER OF THE 2008
NATIONAL HOME BUILDER'S ASSOCIATION
"HOME FOR LIFE" AWARD FOR KITCHENS

A pot filler was installed at the side of the stove to allow for easy access and eliminate the need to reach over the burners. A pull-out spice rack was installed at counter height for easy access. The controls for the vent hood were rewired and installed at under cabinet height for easy access. A pullout, totally accessible, blind cabinet shelving bin was installed in the lower blind corner cabinet. The ovens were lowered for easy access. The microwave was installed at counter height. All lighting was installed in zones with individual control areas, and under cabinet task lighting was installed. Lighting above the cabinets was used to create the illusion of height, and eliminate "dead" and dark spaces. Energy efficient, 12 volt xenon, low voltage concealed linear lighting was utilized as it has a 16,000 hour rating. In addition, lighting was installed in upper glass-front cabinets to highlight the client's collection of art glass.

LifeWise Renovations is dedicated to remodeling homes for every life stage. In this case, they elevated the dishwasher along with the double ovens, enabling use without bending. Several variations of task and general lighting made achieving daily living activities easier.

Variable countertop heights allow people of all heights, shapes, and sizes to work side by side. Contrasting the colors of the countertops with the cabinetry allows for increased visual clarity. The cabinets offer waist-to-shoulder height and easy-to-access storage.

This kitchen offers many time and energy saving features: a gas cook top with front controls, a cutting board between the sink and the cooktop, and the kitchen sink with the garbage disposer in the compartment nearest the cutting board. There is a shelf above the cooktop to store the most frequently used items.

In this mountain home, Pineapple House enclosed the right side of the kitchen island for storage, leaving the left side open so that a wheelchair can fit under it. Compromised vision is a common issue as we age, and its decline generally occurs prior to problems with mobility. While adequate light sources are important throughout the house, especially in a kitchen where sharp tools and hot surfaces are abundant, careful consideration and multiple sources of light and light control are highly recommended. Undercounter task lighting should always be employed. When bright sources are not needed, undercounter lights can be installed with a dimmer to control mood lighting. *Courtesy of Jennifer Lindell Photography.*

The wood-burning fireplace can be used for cooking, warmth, or atmosphere. The hi-tech convection oven under the stone fireplace is a very interesting study in contrasts. The successful union of old and new carries a comfortably positive message. *Courtesy of Jennifer Lindell Photography.*

The gas-top range is framed on three sides by the wooden table/ island. Prep and serving are very easy with this configuration. *Courtesy of Jennifer Lindell Photography.*

BEDROOMS

People spend more time in their bedroom than any other room in the house. As we lose our mobility, flexibility, and eyesight, it makes sense to focus on the safety of the bedroom. Making sure that all furniture is at the correct height and not a trip hazard can be as simple as raising or lowering beds and chairs, moving furniture to create easy access to doorways and closets, and installing better lighting.

The optimum location of the bedroom is on the main level of your home. If that is not possible, building a safe, sturdy staircase is the next step. Continued use of a stair will keep a person fit. A good stair will have treads of a consistent height, handrails on both sides, and contrasting colors on the bottom floor finish. Eventually, physical issues may arise that require the need for a stair lift or elevator.

Clear access through the bedroom and to the bathroom is important. A place to sit and change clothes is useful. Having all bedroom furniture at the correct height is important as we grow older; fortunately, beds today can be adjustable in height. To allow easier access to the bed and reduce the possibility of falling, you might want to install safety rails.

A bedroom should have proper ambient light to illuminate the whole room, but also task lighting at the bed and an even spread of night lighting. The night lighting should create a pathway of light that links the bed to the bathroom and to the stairs so that the path of travel is safe, usable, and does not require additional light to negotiate.

A working phone beside the bed is important for emergencies. Because power outages affect cordless phones, consider adding a phone outlet by your bed and installing a corded phone.

Crowded closets can lead to accidents. If you install a closet system, you can organize your closet more safely while simultaneously creating more access to everything in the closet. Closet light fixtures are relatively inexpensive. You also can find "stick up" lights that are battery powered or lights that turn on and off when the doors are opened or shut. ◆

AN EMPOWERING ENVIRONMENT

A bedroom should be a particularly inviting area. This Pineapple House room offers lots of natural light and three different zones for sitting. Each area has a quality different from the other—one is more conducive to working, another is better for reading and relaxing, while the third zone encourages spending time in front of the fireplace located directly across from the bed. *Courtesy of Scott Moore Photography.*

BARRIER-FREE VIEW

The mullion-free, large-paned doors and windows in this Pineapple House bedroom allow barrier-free views from a lower perspective, such as from the bed or a wheelchair. Two benches are placed at the end of the bed. They can double as ottomans and are a convenient place to put belongings or sit while putting on shoes. Their size makes them easier to move and maneuver than the typical long, single bench seat. *Courtesy of Scott Moore Photography.*

This master bedroom designed by Pineapple House has an attached sleeping porch, which allows the owner to enjoy the fresh air. It is important to use open railing on such a large span of screening, as it does not obstruct the view while it adds a needed barrier and stability to large screened openings. Because they are screened, the double French doors can stay open, and fresh air can freely flow into the primary bedroom, too. A sleeping porch is seasonal and is especially fun during a shower or rainstorm, but there is little audio, climate, or light control outdoors. A ceiling fan helps regulate the temperature while window treatments (such as the roll-up shade shown) assist with privacy and some light exposure. Inside, however, full draw drapery with blackout lining can cover the French doors when total darkness is desired. *Courtesy of Blind Images Photography.*

LifeWise Renovations carried the Italian plaster walls through the master suite to compliment the porcelain tile in the adjoining bathroom. The doorways were widened to accommodate any means of mobility. The installed wood floor has special non-skid finishes that are designed to minimize slipping.

Ensuring that door widths are greater than 32 inches allows access for individuals with mobility issues. Utilizing double doors, pocket doors or off setting hinges are other ways to accomplish this. The free-standing dresser on the left complements the unique built-in dresser on the right. Complete with focused lighting, the dressers offer a unique means to display and accent the homeowner's eclectic collection of artwork. Lighting is an important consideration in increasing the safety and ease of completing daily tasks.

Removing walls tends to make spaces brighter and always makes them easier to navigate. In this beach condo, the Pineapple House designers eliminated the wall that separated the master and its bath, allowing both air and light to flood the formerly dark inner room. The toilet cannot be seen, as it is tucked away in the water closet beyond the shower. Without the dividing wall, the bedroom feels significantly larger and, at every age, is much more enjoyable. *Courtesy of Mon Amour Photography.*

Two sliding barn doors conceal the large entrance to the master bedroom. This style of door allows the resident to pass through the opening without having to deal with the door swing and can completely eliminate the need for a transition strip between the two areas. *Courtesy of Mon Amour Photography.*

Quality barn-style doors move unencumbered across the upper track, making them easy to open and close. The entry and entertainment wall was designed so the doors would completely cover the flat screen television and component/storage closet in the wall below the TV. The homeowners enjoy the surprise expressed by visitors when they move the doors and reveal their hidden, integrated entertainment area. This area is now accessible to them even while in bed. *Courtesy of Mon Amour Photography.*

S. Barzin Architect designed a pull-out clothing rack to be used by an individual in a wheelchair. The use of heavy-duty cabinet sliding brackets allows the cabinet to be pulled out smoothly, without much effort.

Thick baseboards protect the hands on the wheelchair wheels from hitting the wall and also protect the walls from dents caused by the wheelchair.

BATHROOMS

The bathroom is the most important room in the home to render safe and accessible. The first consideration in planning a bathroom is the layout of the toilet, sink, tub, and shower because maneuverability can be a major issue for a senior. Ideally, the bathroom has a large central space, approximately 5 feet in diameter, which allows for a wheelchair, walker, or helper. Each fixture should be approachable directly from this space.

The Sink

The height of the sink counter depends on the user. If a person is in a wheelchair, the sink height should be 34 inches above the finished floor. The depth of the sink basin should be shallow, approximately 6 ½ inches. Knee clearance underneath the sink should be at least 27 inches high and 30 inches wide. The sink should be approachable from the front and have a clear space of 48 x 30 inches, and the chair should be able to roll under. Any exposed pipes under the sink must be insulated and wrapped to prevent accidental contact between a person and hot pipes.

The sink height for a standing person is typically 36 inches. This taller height prevents stooping. If several people with different needs share the sink, it might be worth investing in a motorized sink counter that raises and lowers. The sink cabinet can also be designed as an independent piece, allowing for either the future removal of the base cabinet below for wheelchair access or for conversion to a motorized sink. If planning for wheelchair access, the sink counter should be open underneath.

The sink faucet should have lever handles, not knobs, for turning the water on and off. Manual strength lessens with age, and it is easier to push at a handle than to grasp and turn a knob. When using an undercounter mounted sink, install the lever handles on the side of the sink for easier access instead of knobs at the back.

The mirror should be mounted no higher than 40 inches above the floor. Medicine cabinets behind the sink can become difficult to reach. A more convenient location would be on a sidewall mounted at chest height.

The Tub and Shower

If the space permits, a separate tub and shower provide the most flexibility. A roll in or curb-less shower, with a hand-held shower head, bench, and non-skid floor surface is a user-friendly combination. A separate tub with a low, 16-inch high wall and a wide ledge to sit on when getting in is a nice feature. The shower also should have grab bars on the side and back walls. As grab bars are becoming more common within bathroom renovations, there is expanded choice in the design, color, and length of grab bars, so that they now can blend into the overall decorative scheme for the bathroom. If the tub and shower are combined, one can adjust a few things to make it easier to step into the shower. A tub unit with a door is another option. If a soaking tub is desired, units with doors are available.

Another way to increase the user-friendly aspect of a tub is to build a wide surround that can be used as a bench. The user can sit down and then swing his/her legs across to get into the tub, instead of standing at the tub and trying to step into it.

The shower should have grab bars installed directly into the studs. Flip-down shower seats provide space for a caregiver to stand while assisting with transfers. If a bathtub is not required, a direct access or roll in shower is a good solution because it eliminates the need to step over a raised threshold. The moment of the step up is a critical chance to lose one's balance.

A hand-held shower head increases the flexibility of washing. It also creates the ability to wash while seated, if a chair or bench is available. The floor surface should be slip resistant. Today, it is

Pineapple House designed this door-less flush-entry shower located at the end of a hallway with a radius wide enough for a wheelchair to pivot. The distance of the water source from the entry of the tiled enclosure makes a door and transition strip unnecessary. The honed small tile pattern gives easy traction. The handles and hand-held shower are mounted low enough for easy access when sitting. The built-in bench seat is positioned so a complete shower is possible even if the person is sitting on it. *Courtesy of Gary Langhammer Studios.*

Neville Architecture, working with Patrick's Residential Management Services as the builder, designed this shower, blending modern with nautical. The tiled flooring flows out of the shower and past the frameless door. The bench and hand held shower wand add convenience. The linear drain detail along the back edge eliminates the need to slope the floor towards a center drain, keeping the floor more level. The tile inset is a nautical chart of Narragansett Bay, Rhode Island, provided by Weatherly Tile, Portsmouth, Rhode Island.

possible to buy prefabricated tub/showers that have the handrails, bench, and non-skid surface already installed.

Showers and tubs are now made with integral non-skid surfaces, which may be rough faced stone, patterns of stones, or mosaics with a tight grout pattern.

Toilet

The ADA toilet seat height is between 17 and 19 inches, which is higher than standard residential height. The extra height makes it easier to rise to a standing position. Individual grab bars can also be installed to either side of the toilet. The toilet should be set in a corner with grab bars behind and to one side, so a person can approach from the front or the side.

Grab Bars

Grab bars offer stability and guidance. A grab bar in the bathtub helps with stepping up and into the tub and lowering the body down. A grab bar at the toilet assists with lowering and raising one's body up and down, helping to maintain balance in a moment of transition.

The proper positioning of grab bars is essential since they can be used unexpectedly and with full body weight. Because of the dual use, proper installation is very important; the bar needs to carry a person's weight and also their weight at the moment of falling, a force that can be twice the normal weight. A licensed contractor who knows how to properly fasten the bars into the structural studs of the wall should install all grab bars.

A towel rod cannot be used as a grab bar because it does not have the strength to carry an adult person's weight. When installing towel rods in the bathroom, choose sturdy rods and have them properly installed into the wall with supports added directly to the studs. When someone stumbles, they'll grab at anything. At the age of 12, my sister slipped in the shower. She fell, grabbing at the built-in tile washcloth bar. The bar was at a convenient height and easy to grab, but it was designed to hold the weight of a small damp towel. Clearly, it could not hold up a 100-pound frantic adolescent. Her jerking motion against the bar not only dislodged the bar from the wall, it also took with it the fifteen surrounding tiles, landing my sister, wet and bruised, in a pile of moldy tiles and thirty year-old wallboard. At a young age, I learned that anyone can fall in the shower, no matter what age and how agile.

Doorways

An easy way to gain extra space in the bathroom is to have the door swing out, freeing up the interior bathroom space. Narrow doorways can be a constraint for someone using a wheelchair or walker, but they can be widened during renovation. Another option is to replace the existing hinges with an expandable offset door hinge. These hinges allow the door to swing clear of the door opening, gaining approximately 2 inches of additional clearance. As with faucet hardware, it's best to choose levered door handles instead of traditional knobs, so that older hands can continue to easily operate the door hardware.

Lighting

Good lighting at the sink helps with personal grooming, such as brushing teeth, putting on makeup, or combing hair. Task lighting at the bathroom sink can be sconces, pendants, or recessed lighting above the mirror. When planning a general overhead light, look for a fixture that is a multi-purpose light, fan, and/or heat lamp. In the shower or bathing area install a recessed waterproof light fixture.

A creative approach to non-slip floor surfaces is shown in this Patrick's Residential Management Services project, with a pebble surface floor for the main bathroom space and a wooden lattice flooring inserted into the shower. The shower has a matching wooden free standing bench and handheld nozzle.

Designed by Neville Architecture, the standard Kohler tub shown has integral grab bars. The owners wanted further support. A vertical grab bar and a diagonal grab bar were mounted directly into the shower walls. These extra bars offer support when standing in the shower and provide more leverage when getting out of the tub.

Heat

Regulating a person's body heat can make a big difference in the comfort level at home. The transition of wet to dry in the bathroom is the strongest test on a body for maintaining a constant body temperature. A few items can be installed to help. My personal favorite is a towel warmer, which can be electric plug-in units or hard-wired directly. A warm towel helps prevent a body from losing too much heat after a shower. Another option is a heat lamp fixture to keep the overall temperature of the room higher than that of the rest of the house. Radiant flooring also maintains a warm and comfortable temperature in the bathroom, again creating an environment that will make the space comfortable. All of these heating suggestions can be installed with timers to regulate their use and increase their efficiency.

Cabinetry

Bathroom storage and cabinetry have similar requirements as that of the kitchen. Chest to shoulder height cabinets are the ideal height. A medicine cabinet at the back of the sink can be difficult to stretch towards. Consider finding an alternative location like a sidewall or use storage in drawers of a base cabinet. Another possibility is bifold doors at closets. ◆

In this bathroom designed by Pineapple House, the vanity has room for knee clearance if a wheelchair needs to roll under it. There are five sources of light for the sink: the candlestick lamp, the sconces, the task lighting near the molding, the overhead light, and the mirrors that reflect the daylight from the windows across the room. *Courtesy of Scott Moore Photography.*

The glass block wall, shown in this bathroom designed by Neville Architecture, helps share light across the expanse of the entire bathroom.

A heated towel rod is a wonderful luxury.

Deep River Partners designed a tranquil retreat within the residence that does not sacrifice style for function. The deck-mounted tub creates an easy seat and swing into the tub. An elliptical ceiling soffit with integrated cove lighting unifies the circular shower with the rest of the room. The skylight above the whirlpool floods the room with natural light, providing visual clarity. Expansive uninterrupted floor area allows for easy movement. The "comfort height" toilet provides an elevated seat, reducing leg stress. Contrasting floor and wall tile emphasize a visual separation between the horizontal and vertical planes for easy navigation. The calm and soothing color palette, scented candles, and chromotherapy tub reinforce this spa-like experience within the home. *Courtesy of Joe De Maio.*

Universal accessibility is maximized at the master shower with a curb-less threshold and door-less entry. Decorative glass block walls allow natural light to bathe the master shower while creating privacy to the outdoors. Muted stone and tile selections coincide with the serene feel of the space, while decorative tile mosaics add detail. The cracked tile floor provides slip resistance and presents a visual cue to the wet area. Warmth is provided through radiant floors and heated towel racks—the racks are within easy reach. One can adjust the showering experience by utilizing the rain head, shower head, or hand shower. The cantilevered seat offers a respite while showering and is easy to clean. *Courtesy of Joe De Maio.*

The dressing room uses a curved backlit wall that frames the Zen-like natural branch structure and artistic vase. The architects at Deep River Partners utilized an axial alignment to the bath from the dressing room, creating a clear connection. An indirect overhead light cove provides ambient illumination free from disruptive shadowing and glare. A cushioned bench completes the central focus and provides functionality while dressing. *Courtesy of Joe De Maio.*

Added elegance is achieved by integrating a pedestal sink with flanking chest-like cabinets. The framed mirror opens as a medicine chest, complete with electric outlets. The Deep River team employed a ledge for further convenience, adding to the soft style and underscoring the spa-like feel. Wall sconces flank the mirror, providing superior task illumination and eliminating harsh shadows while grooming. Down lights adequately light the counters to either side. *Courtesy of Joe De Maio.*

THE BATHROOM

Roxane Carson Designs used a large, recessed mirrored medicine cabinet, a comfort height, elongated toilet, easy-to-reach towel bar, and single-lever faucet, along with grab bar ready walls. Additional structural blocking has been installed in walls, and grab bars can be installed when needed.

Although small in size, this powder room has ample natural light and plenty of space to move about because of the tall pedestal sink.

The monochromatic sand tone of the fixtures and floor increases warmth in the room. A non-slip, honed, travertine tile set in the "Versailles" pattern adds texture, durability, and understated luxury.

Carolyn Cook of LiveSmart Design knows that the bathroom is where most falls occur in the home. Her renovated bathroom is a great example of how a room can be both beautiful and functional. She took a typical 5 x 7 foot bathroom and made it three times larger by absorbing underutilized space from closets and hallways and removing walls. A 5-foot opening, with double pocket-doors, enhances the view from the bedroom while providing easy access for mobility devices. Up-lighting fixtures mounted on each side of the mirror provide balanced lighting on the face and prevent glare from a seated position. The single lever handle at the lavatory is perfect for arthritic hands. The cabinetry can easily adjust in the future for wheelchair use by the homeowner if needed. The front doors and toe kick of the sink cabinet can be removed for access.

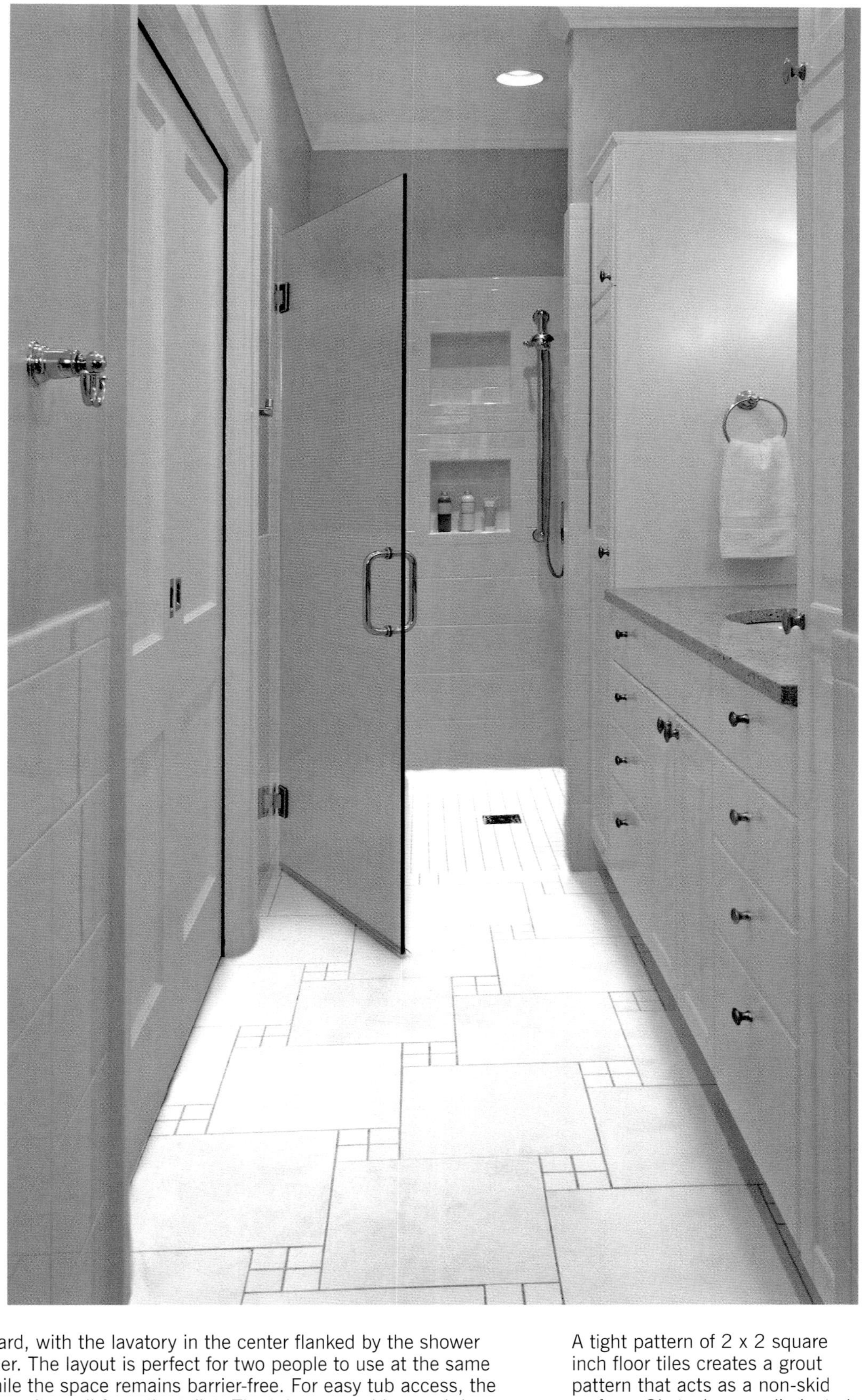

This bathroom floor plan is straightforward, with the lavatory in the center flanked by the shower on one end and the toilet/tub on the other. The layout is perfect for two people to use at the same time. The wing wall provides privacy while the space remains barrier-free. For easy tub access, the spout and controls are located on the opposite wall from the toilet. The tub surround has grab bars on three sides, and grab bars support towels. Towel bars are the first thing people reach for when falling so it's best to either replace them with grab bars or install them like grab bars.

Safety and ease of maintenance are concerns for the aging homeowner. The pivoting shower door has patterned glass instead of clear, which makes cleaning easier and hides toiletries from view. The curb-less shower is excellent for wheeled traffic and eliminates nooks and crannies where dirt can hide. Semi-gloss paint wipes clean and helps prevent the growth of mold and mildew. Darker grout with white tile requires less elbow grease and defines the tile pattern nicely.

A tight pattern of 2 x 2 square inch floor tiles creates a grout pattern that acts as a non-skid surface. Obstacles are eliminated by placing toiletries in recessed niches and laundry/trash in pull-out bins. The shower door swings out to assist a fallen person, while a handheld shower on a slider/grab bar prevents falling in the first place.

"We need a bathroom that is 'user-friendly'!" said the clients about their existing bathroom, shown here. They didn't want to have to worry about trying to get into the shower or tub if and when they became less agile. They also didn't want a bathroom that looked institutional. Grab bars were not needed at this time, but they wanted to be able to install them at a later date if they became necessary.

In the course of providing a "user-friendly" and aesthetically pleasing space, Leslie Shankman-Cohen of Jill Hertz Interior Design implemented Universal Design and green/sustainable design strategies throughout the project. She took into account smooth floor transitions, possible future use of wheelchair or other mobility devices, accessible cabinets, sustainable, renewable, and green products, energy efficiency, and resale values.

The shower was gutted and replaced with a curb-less, roll–in shower with frameless glass doors. The entire shower area was blocked all around up to a 48-inch height for future installation of grab bars. The shower floor is made from smooth shaved rock to give an upscale, spa-like appearance without any slipping hazards.

Asian influenced custom cabinets were designed and installed, with "his" side being at a higher level to accommodate his six foot two inch stature. Upper cabinets were also installed to house electrical appliances for an easy to reach, "already plugged in" access.

The slick man-made marble landing pads in front of the shower and tub were removed and replaced with textured tiles. A border of shaved rock around the tub deck, on the floor in front of the tub and continuing in front of each vanity adds to the spa-like feeling.

To allow for more light penetration into the water closet and two walk-in clothes closets, the original doors were replaced with custom doors with glass inserts and rice paper film covering the glass to give the essence of shoji screens. Privacy screens made of bamboo imbedded in acrylic are hung between the vanities and the tub to embellish the Zen feeling.

This lake cottage bath sports an easy to clean beadboard wall surface, which also illuminates the room. Roxane Carson Designs added a lighted rocker switch and programmable fan timer for easy access and carefree exit. A LED night-light shows the way for young and old alike. Easy grip cup pulls and "C" door pulls adorn the vanity along with an integral sink and single lever faucet with anti-scald mechanism.

The designer used high contrast surfaces to make navigation easier on aging eyes. A commode cabinet for extra storage sits above the comfort height elongated toilet. A porcelain tiled shower stall is equipped with a curved shower rod to add comfortable elbow room. The walls are coated with VOC-free paint, and the non-vinyl liner curtain also emits no VOCs.

The radiant in-floor heat helps keep the ambient temperature of the room warm and warms the inhabitants' bare feet. The tub deck is 18 inches high for wheelchair height access, and the tub has integral armrests. The shower head uses a single lever faucet, and shampoo niches are found at two different heights at the back of the tub area.

Under-stair space adjacent to this bathroom is not wasted. The pocket door at the left hides a storage area and laundry hampers. Built-in shelves house baskets containing towels, washcloths, toilet paper, and other bath supplies.

THE BATHROOM

Green Construction Services completed a bathroom remodel for a Vietnam War veteran in Florida. Awarded a Purple Heart and a Silver Star after his tour of duty, the veteran *needed* the space to be wheelchair accessible but also desired an attractive bathroom suite design that would aesthetically blend into the home's existing surroundings. *Courtesy of Sandra A. Johnson.*

The project included the removal of a spa tub, the deck and steps into the tub, the removal of the 6-inch curb into the shower, as well as the replacement of narrow entryways into the toilet room and shower area. To coordinate the newly remodeled bathroom suite with the existing master bedroom, new tile was selected and installed to coordinate the two rooms. *Courtesy of Sandra A. Johnson.*

Matching his and her cabinetry allows for equitable use as well as an aesthetically pleasing and unifying look. The handicap-accessible vanity includes knee-guard cabinetry under his open vanity, which features an 18 inch drawer unit and matches the closed cabinetry under her vanity. The drawers allow ample storage space and easy access. *Courtesy of Sandra A. Johnson.*

Her vanity mirrors his vanity, but contains closed cabinetry and appealing furniture-style features. Both vanities feature granite countertops, new wall-mounted light fixtures, and two GFCI outlets. *Courtesy of Sandra A. Johnson.*

MBC Building & Remodeling, LLC built an aesthetically pleasing bathroom. From left to right, top to bottom, this bath was designed to please the eye and help the homeowner stay in their home for the long term. A higher, comfort style toilet is sequestered nicely behind a half wall. *Courtesy of Heather A. Johnson.*

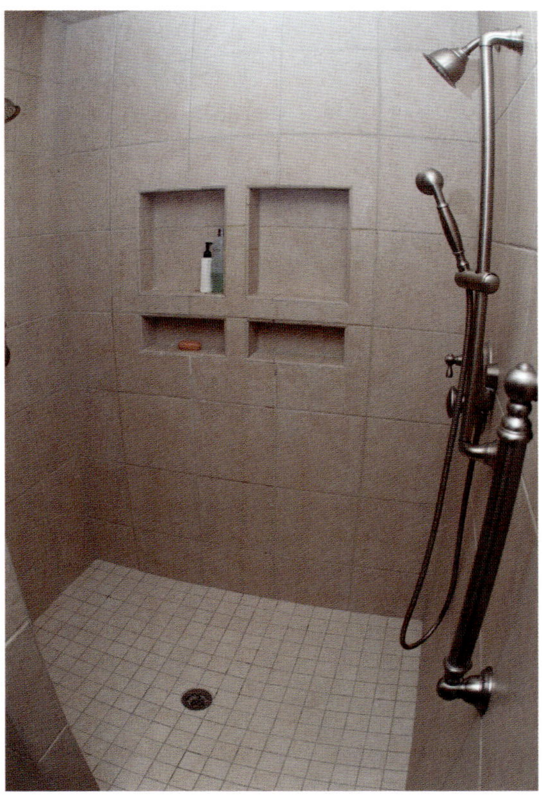

The large, no curb shower allows the homeowners the opportunity for graceful aging in their own bathroom. *Courtesy of Heather A. Johnson.*

Multiple designer hand bars were used, including one that doubled as a shower head holder. A seat was also built into the custom shower stall. *Courtesy of Heather A. Johnson.*

This gorgeous, custom, full-light, glass pocket door was installed for its beauty and function. Before one enters the space—expect something special!

A double, raised height, maple vanity with undermount sinks was specified for this space. Each side of the vanity has a single-lever faucet, "C" drawer pulls, and tilt-out trays for hidden storage. Husband and wife have their own recessed, mirrored medicine cabinets for more cherished storage area. The comfort height toilet has a commode cabinet above it and a "grab bar ready" wall next to it.

The focal point of decadence in this Roxane Carson Designs' bathroom is the heated, bubble massage tub, which is already equipped with stylish grab bars above and next to the tub.

Another "Wave" style grab bar graces the shower stall and is beneficial for the occupant of the corner shower bench.

The frameless, glass-enclosed shower stall was made possible by demolishing two small linen closets. The door swings in and out to facilitate an easy entrance and exit. It features two shampoo niches and a sliding bar shower spray head to accommodate a standing or a seated user. The honed 2-inch square Travertine tiles on the shower floor provide a non-slip surface.

Control Center! Rocker switches for lights and heat lamps, programmable fan timer, and ground fault interrupter make life easy, comfortable, and safe.

RED Interior created an adapted bathroom for a grandmother who had a knee replacement and occasionally used a cane. A sit-down vanity area, while luxurious, is also a useful feature for those experiencing poorer balance and reduced flexibility. This traditional design offers hot and cold levers and an undermount sink for easy use and cleaning. Pull-out drawers beneath sinks are an excellent adaptation for easy access and storage.

The walk-in shower has minimal lip and enough room for a shower chair or stool. This design offers bracing already installed behind the walls for grab bars for future use if necessary. An overhead shower head and hand held shower is ideal for whether standing or seated. The patterned 1 x 5 inch mosaic floor tile is an elegant way to provide slip-resistant flooring both inside and outside of the shower.

This view looks at the steam shower with its European obscure glass door. Separate his and hers vanities, adorned with stone countertops and china undermount sinks, maximizes functionality. Organized accessible storage is achieved by combining the vanities with a large walk-in closet. The floor outside the steam shower is enhanced by an electric floor-warming element that keeps the entire suite cozy and comfortable on cold, Midwestern winter mornings. The bidet offers that European flair.

LifeWise Renovations removed existing black variegated marble material and replaced it with warm and rich Tuscan-style porcelain tile, adding a feeling of luxury and comfort. A step was installed to aid maneuvering in and out of the tub. The comfort height toilet allows for ease of access while maintaining a sleek and stylish look.

The steam shower view has a flip-up/flip-down teak seat. A full-shower steam unit comparable to any high end spa compliments the polished chrome Moen fixtures. The location of the controls and hand-held shower allow the user to be seated while adjusting the temperature and spray settings.

The master bathroom steam shower entrance highlights barrier-free access with the shower floor tile and bathroom floor tile set in the same plane. Utilizing state-of-the-art technology from Europe, the barrier-free base replaces the existing wood subfloor. It is not only safer, but creates a smooth modern look.

The clients' master bath was small, dated, and in need of some TLC. They no longer enjoyed taking baths and wanted to simplify to a shower unit only. Although addressing accessibility was not an immediate concern, the owners wanted to make their master bath feel more open, easier to clean, and have the potential of future accessibility modifications. Although there was no room to expand the footprint of the area and the budget was tight, Leslie Shankman-Cohen of Jill Hertz Interior Design resolved many of their issues with her renovation design. The use of white tiles with small areas of accent color made the small space feel large.

The tub was gutted and replaced with a curb-less, roll-in shower with frameless glass partition. The entire shower area was blocked all around up to a 48-inch height for future installation of grab bars. A simple glass partition keeps the water from splashing into the vanity area, and the shower and floor are arranged in such a way that minimal water sprays out of the shower area.

The wall tiles extend onto the floor, giving the illusion of a more uniform and continuous space. Glass tiles, 1-inch square, were used to give a more decorative feel. The clear glass partition also helps give the illusion of a more open space.

The existing vanity was reused, repainted, and raised to give a more comfortable height for the homeowner. More energy efficient lighting was installed which also improved the light quality. A lower, inefficient toilet was replaced with a water efficient, comfort height toilet.

When his wife suffered a crippling illness that necessitated a wheelchair, the client hired Green Construction Services to remodel the master bathroom to be completely handicap accessible. The firm doubled the existing space from 37 square feet to 60 square feet. The firm replaced the 24-inch doorway and narrow hallways with a 36-inch door for wheelchair access. *Courtesy of Sandra A. Johnson.*

The previous shower had an 8 inch curb and 24 inch opening. The remodel included a handicap-accessible shower with the addition of a bench, fixed and removable shower heads, and mounted grab bars. *Courtesy of Sandra A. Johnson.*

The old bathroom featured a 21 inch wall-mounted sink, which did not allow wheelchair access. Green Construction Services installed a new vanity with scald-guard protection and a bank of drawers for storage. Angled cabinetry conceals the plumbing. *Courtesy of Sandra A. Johnson.*

After a refreshing dip in the lake, it won't matter if your feet are still wet. Open the lever-handled, 36 inch door in this lakeshore cabin and walk right into the low threshold shower that is clad in durable, non-skid porcelain and beautiful natural travertine tiles. Find shampoo and soap in one of the two built-in niches. A central vacuum will clean up any errant sand on the floor.

Visual acuity is assisted through the use of high contrast surfaces in this Roxane Carson Designs' bathroom. The light, seamless counter top with integral sink is juxtaposed with the black, distressed vanity and the sand colored floor. Cup drawer pulls along with the single lever faucet lend an easy grip for the occupant.

An illuminated rocker light switch and a programmable fan timer help to navigate in the dark, save money, and aid with forgetfulness. An additional LED night-light is hard-wired next to the vanity just above floor level to light the way at night. The easy-to-reach towel ring keeps the hand towel dry and convenient.

A combination of good universal design elements, this bathroom has a comfort height elongated toilet, a commode cabinet for storage, and an additional mirror to reflect and magnify light in the windowless space. The toilet walls are grab bar ready with additional structural blocking within the walls.

A corner bench is a great place to rest while shaving or showering and there is no need to clean glass or wash curtains in this door-less shower stall.

Just outside the shower, experience the wonderful luxury of a towel warmer! On your way out, hang your robe on the handy, door-mounted robe hook.

LifeWise Renovations designed this guest bathroom with a 12 x 12 inch porcelain veined floor laid in a parquet pattern for a visually appealing and lively contrast. Visual contrast can also help individuals with low vision to maneuver with increased safety.

Additional visual interest is achieved by laying the porcelain tile in a vertical running bond pattern that is accented by the glass tile stripe inside the shower.

Safety is maximized by installing a floor surface that is non-slip and barrier-free.

S. Barzin Architect designed a cantilevered sink and tilted mirror to provide easy access to the sink. The exposed plumbing will be covered soon.

The no-threshold shower area is separated from the rest of the bathroom by a simple curtain. Colored tiles trimming the edges clearly define the perimeters of the room. The entire subfloor of the bathroom is waterproofed and sloped to the drain.

OUTDOOR SPACES

The various paths of travel throughout your property should meet a few minimum requirements. Is the walk smooth and without unexpected bumps? Is the path evenly lit? Is the path wide enough for you to walk comfortably? At stairs, are there handrails? The transition from outside to inside should be convenient, safe, and familiar.

Initially, you should review the route from the street to the front door, from the garage to the back door, and any shortcuts through the back or side yard. Consider how visitors approach the house and which entry you use on a regular basis and then reflect on its friendliness. Think back and review the places you or someone else has fallen or tripped. Survey those areas and think about what could make the area safer. Handrails should be added to outdoor stairs. Even stairs that are just one or two steps can cause hesitation, if there is nothing to hold onto for balance. Inclement weather can make those areas especially hazardous.

Look for bumps, cracks, or other changes in materials along your route. Material changes, such as walking from a concrete driveway to a brick walkway, can be problematic because they are often accompanied by a change in height, color, or uneven surface. More than a ¼ inch level change can be hazardous and is defined as a trip hazard by the Americans with Disabilities Act. Maybe the bricks need to be recessed further into the dirt, or perhaps a new set of bricks is needed if they are chipped. Is the area shady, making it hard to see the walkway surface? Decide how better to light the area, either by pruning nearby bushes and trees or installing additional exterior task lighting.

Often there is a certain presentational quality to the front entry and a relaxed haphazard aura to the back door entry. Ideally, all entrances to the house should be safe and accommodating to enter. Remember that the entry you use the most at the present time might not be the entry that will be the most accommodating as your needs change. The back door, the entry that you currently hop into every night from the garage might be in a space that is quite narrow while the front door may have a covered entry and a wider path.

Questions to ask:

- Is the path at least 36 inches wide at all locations?
- Is the path well lit along its entire length?
- Is the material of the path smooth and consistent?
- Is there a handrail at ramped areas?
- Is there a handrail at the stairs?
- Does the drainage along the path work well?

The Path

Modifications to your home should start at the property line. In a commercial, public, or institutional building, the minimum width of the path of travel generally ranges between 48 to 60 inches. Its width depends on the number of people expected to use the space, the direction of the door swing, and the building's use. In a residential environment, the width of these standards feels either luxurious or impersona!. A wheelchair can comfortably move on a 36 inch wide path, but a person would have trouble passing the wheelchair if unable to step outside the path's limits. If the wheelchair has to turn, additional space IS needed, and the recommendation is a 5 foot wide turning circle. The dimensions discussed here are for residential use only and should be considered guidelines.

At intersections of material changes, such as brick meeting concrete, create a flat, smooth transition. A variety of thresholds can be purchased to help slope the transition from outside to inside at doorways. Along exterior paths, it is best to minimize the material changes and repair areas that have a bumpy surface in excess of ¼ inch.

Naomi Neville points out, "These are good examples using different materials in interesting ways to liven up a path. All the materials are flush to one another and well maintained so they do not cause a trip hazard."

The Railing

A well-designed railing creates a friendly path both for the inhabitant and the occasional visitor. A continuous handrail is not required on a straight, flat path, but in areas where the elevation changes. The railing is not merely used as a walking aid over difficult terrain but to expand the user's confidence and to allow them to maintain their balance.

The amount and style of railing added both inside and outside a home is a personal choice. A comfortable height for a handrail is between 34–38 inches. The handrail should have a 1-½ inch diameter so that it can be grabbed firmly. These recommendations may not suit the character of the house or the occupant, and a more creative approach may be necessary. A professional contractor should install the handrail to the building or into the ground.

A guardrail is not to be confused with a handrail. A guardrail should be added to any spot that has a drop off of more than 30 inches, e.g., along the perimeter of an elevated porch. Adding guardrails or an object that acts like a guardrail is a good idea, even if the grade change is less than 30 inches. Any fall can be troubling to weak knees. Assess potential problem areas that might cause falling or tripping off an elevated surface. Not all areas will mandate a guardrail as the solution and instead creative ideas such as planters, benches, or garden elements might also be used as a way to direct the flow of traffic and block problem areas.

The Steps

The first floor of a house is raised off the ground to prevent flooding, deter unwanted rodents, and create basement space. Even in sunny dry climates, such as southern California, the narrow ventilation crawl space under the house raises the first floor above the ground just enough to require steps.

The two to five steps that lead up to the front door can be the most treacherous element of a house. These steps are often uneven in height, crooked, and cracked. They can be made from a variety of materials, which deteriorate over time, creating obstacles such as broken concrete with weeds or loose boards. How many times have we seen a thin iron railing haphazardly attached to a wall extending halfway down the steps? Or worse, a free-standing railing, connected in two places by thin, 50-year-old iron fasteners, swaying when grasped, belying its credibility as a useful hand railing.

At a minimum, stairs should have a handrail on one side. It should extend past the last step at least 12 inches. A standard rule of thumb for stair design is an 11 inch tread and a 7 inch riser. Lengthening the step's tread is acceptable but don't increase the height of the risers. Over time people become adjusted to the standards of stair heights and deviating the height or narrowing the tread causes problems.

At the base of the stairs, contrast the color of the walkway with that of the treads to help to avoid the confusion of whether or not the last step has been reached. An older person can often have trouble with depth perception, which is why there is often hesitation by an older person when stepping down at the end of a staircase.

Ideally, steps leading up to the entry are covered overhead. Rain and especially snow can make a routine trip to the driveway difficult. Inclement weather also causes haste, which in turn can cause a needless stumble.

"Here," Naomi Neville says, "the steps are built into the landscape to get you down the hill, and the brick connects smoothly to the concrete at the top and bottom. The decorative handrails are both attractive and functional."

The small flower urns are a simple way to decorate the rail and place it in the landscape.

The Ramp

Most people do not require a ramp, but if you do, spend the time and money to build a safe ramp. In the planning stage, map out possible locations. Measure the change in height from entry to the exterior grade. The slope of the ramp should not exceed a 1:12 height to length ratio. Allocate at least a 5 foot diameter platform at the top and bottom of the ramp. The handrail should extend past the sloped portion by at least 12 inches in both directions. The length of the ramp should not exceed 30 feet and the width should be 36 inches as measured between the handrails. Keep the ramp straight and the slope constant. Continuous handrails should be placed on both sides. The surface of the ramp must be a non-skid material. Remember that when it rains on the ramp, it will be very slippery, both for the person in the wheelchair and the person guiding the chair.

The Entry Platform

Once you've reached the elevation of the entrance, there is some creativity in the approach to the front door. Ideally, the entry porch is generous enough to allow for a full 180 degree swing of either a screen or main door. There should be enough space to back up out of the way of the swing. A landing with a clear space of 5 feet in diameter is the minimum suggested size. Be generous in planning this space; you do not want to feel nervous about standing at the edge of the entry, leaning out over the few steps you just managed to get up.

As we have all experienced, it is hard to find keys, open the screen door, insert the key into the lock, and turn the handle while holding a grocery bag. A piece of furniture, such as a bench or a table allows you to conveniently set the bag down until the door is open. The furniture can also be used for storage.

Exterior Surfaces

Walkways leading from the driveway to the door, the door to the garage, to the trash/recycling bins, and to the garden are all surfaces that get frequent use. Unexpected falls can occur when materials change, such as a transition from a brick walkway to a concrete walkway, and their intersections are bumpy or not well lit. Even color change can cause hesitation. So when planning material changes along exterior walkways, which is important for the aesthetics and maintenance of a garden landscape, carefully consider the material change locations, their construction and the long term maintenance plan.

A curb a few inches higher than the walkway surface can define the edges of the walkway path, helping a wheelchair, cane, or walker to stay on course. The use of fine gravel or stone dust is acceptable for garden paths though they will require more maintenance to keep them smooth and weed free. Remember it is the transition of materials—not so much the material itself—that can cause the problems.

Lighting

Modifying the interior and exterior lighting can be one of the most useful and beneficial modifications to make your home safer for older adults. Light is needed to see the tiny keyhole in the lock when arriving home late. Lights are needed to see the walkway in from the driveway. Lights are needed to exit the house, and light illuminates the often-used exterior spaces such as the garage. Lights are needed for visitors to safely arrive and depart the house. Security lights are needed to view the extent of the property in case there is an unexplained noise. When you are younger, stumbling in the dark to take out the garbage is irritating but not threatening. A pair of young eyes can adjust

In his landscaping design, S. Barzin Architect avoided the construction of an 18-foot long ramp structure by sloping the walkway and the patio by 5 percent. A very short ramp was provided at the end of the patio onto the rear deck and entry to the house. The raised flower beds inside the wooden barrels allow the individual in the wheelchair to attend to simple gardening.

quickly to the flash of an exposed bulb turning on in the garage. When older, a sharp contrast in light levels can be painful and temporarily blinding.

The varied lighting requirements demand a mix of light fixture types and also a mix of switching methods for the fixtures. Most houses will have a front door light that either needs to be manually turned on or is light sensitive, meaning that it will turn on automatically when the ambient light level goes below a preset limit. At a minimum, there should be a light at each entrance to the house and garage. Because these lights do not need to be on at all times, they can be placed on a motion detector or a light sensitive system. Motion detector lights are often preferred because of the cost savings resulting from them not being on all night. A three-way switch can be installed that allows one to turn the lights on at the base of the driveway or at the garage so that there is control over the lights at each end. If a friend stops to visit, the lights can be turned on from inside. The switch outside is convenient because you may go out in the day and return after dark. The lights can also be set to turn on with a timer. However you choose to control the lights, the added illumination will help the feeling of security when entering or leaving the house at night.

Lights at destination spots are a minimum requirement. Ideally, the entire path of travel would be evenly illuminated so that you can walk comfortably without tripping and stumbling. Landscape lights can be added flush to the ground if there is a hardscape walkway. They can be added to the side of the house, on the garage, or on installed poles. Step lights can be a worthwhile investment for houses that have a series of steps that must be negotiated.

The switching for these lights is important. Just flipping on the lights by a switch at the fixture while outside is not the best. Older eyes will be adjusted to low light levels, and a fast change in light level can be blinding. Before leaving the house, the lights on the path should be on so that there is never an abrupt change in light level. These lights can be on a dimmer switch, as can the interior hall lights, so at night, the eyes can already be adjusted to lower light levels both in the house and on the path. When at the garage, these lights should match the illumination of the path and be gradually brightened for a specific task. ◆

The iron design of this ramp matches the existing style of the decorative iron railings of the house, at the Jekyll Island Club Hotel.

This ramp also at the Jekyll Island Club Hotel in Georgia is coordinated with existing porch railing and the colors of the house, which pulls the design together. Up close, you see the modern handrail tucked along the side.

Changing the color and the material can define a walkway, but do ensure that the transitions are smooth and well maintained.

Neville Architecture designed a sun porch with lights along the length of the house to illuminate the path from the driveway to the entry. *Courtesy of Meghan Sepe.*

This configuration designed by Pineapple House in Florida uses huge screened panels to create an outdoor paradise that allows a less-mobile person to be a part of the action without having to travel far or cross difficult terrain. An outdoor kitchen/grilling area supports al fresco dining and ensures that social experiences will occur in the oasis. Gatherings are opportunities to make memories and share laughs with family and friends. Laughter is one of the best gifts one can bring to a senior. *Courtesy of Jennifer Lindell Photography.*

Modern elements like a television and fireplace will draw people outdoors, where other dimensions of the environment, like fresh air, can also be experienced. Note the stool in front of the lounge chair for resting tired legs. *Courtesy of Jennifer Lindell Photography.*

Along the length of the covered entry porch, there are benches on either side of the door to put down the bags or sit and enjoy the view. The central space provides ample access, allowing the screen door to open fully without crowding the landing. The porch is covered from the elements so snow and rain do not beat down on the front door. The interior space is lit with the low winter southern light and the deep eave overhangs block the intense summer light. *Courtesy of Meghan Sepe.*

This entry porch designed by Neville Architecture has a double-sided handrail for climbing the stairs. *Courtesy of Meghan Sepe.*

Nature, visual stimuli, and fresh air can draw people outdoors, sparking brain activity and increasing circulation. Stephen Hatcher created a deck with curved edges and a rail with acrylic panels to allow an unobstructed view of Oyster Bay, Washington. The deck is made from pressure-treated fir posts and plywood with a waterproof non-slip surface. The rail is made from Sunwood® treated lumber cut into laminates that were glued together to form the curves. Steve says, "As we grow older, this area of the deck is the focus of gatherings with friends, as well as an excellent viewpoint to watch the changing seasons, bird migrations, and sea kayakers."

Pineapple House designers point out that pools and hot tubs offer physical benefits to all ages. Swimming is a lifetime sport that works the heart, lungs, and muscles with very little joint strain. Sometimes it is the only exercise or therapy a person can do if they are weak or have an injury. The muscle relaxing and joint loosening properties from regular exposure to hot circulating water in a hot tub is said to help those with conditions like arthritis, carpal tunnel syndrome, fibromyalgia, tendonitis, scoliosis, and bursitis. Water environments are great assets in a home where aging in place is considered. *Courtesy of Jennifer Lindell Photography.*

Behind the fence lies a pool designed by Neville Architecture for a home on Shelter Island. The goal was to screen it so it blends perfectly into the landscape while simultaneously creating the physical activity benefits of a pool and the walking path that surrounds the perimeter.

This pool, designed by Newport landscape architect Tanya Kelley of PLACEstudio, focuses on the health benefits of a pool for the body and mind. The setting is secluded and relaxing, built into a rocky outcropping and preserving the natural landscaping. The pool itself has a safe and secure entry, with steps and a railing into the main pool for lap swimming, and a separate hot tub pool area, with its own set of steps and bench. The owner, who has impaired mobility due to severe arthritis, uses the pool every day during the spring and summer months.

BIBLIOGRAPHY AND HONORS

Allen Associates

Edminster, Ann. *Energy Free: Homes for a Small Planet.* San Rafael, CA: Green Building Press, 2009.

Johnston, David and Scott Gibson. *Toward a Zero Energy Home.* Newtown, CT: The Taunton Press, Inc., 2010.

Roberts, Jennifer. *Good Green Homes: Creating Better Homes for a Healthier Planet*. Layton, UT: Gibbs Smith, 2003.

Honors

Recipient of the Contractor of the Year Award from the Santa Barbara Contractors Association in 2000, 2003, and 2004.

Selected as one of the Top 8 Innovative Builders in the US, Recognized by *Professional Remodeler Magazine*, 2007.

Recipient of two Santa Barbara County "Green Awards," recognizing exceptional environmental businesses.

Brion Jeanette Architecture

Flowers, Susan. "Innovative Design Meets Sustainability," *Luxury Home Quarterly Magazine*, 2011.

Matthews, Kelly. "Shedding Light on Sustainable Architecture," *Bask Magazine*, 2011.

Rooney, E. Ashley. *Asian Influenced Architecture & Design*. Atglen, PA: Schiffer Publishing, Ltd., 2010.

Brock Rubina Architects

Barnes, Christine. *Before and After Bathroom Makeovers.* Menlo Park, CA: Oxmoor House, 2006.

Rooney, E. Ashley. *Cliffhangers & Hillside Houses.* Atglen, PA: Schiffer Publishing, Ltd., 2006.

Brusco Design & Renovation

Aromin, Joshua. "Staying Home," *Rhode Island Monthly: Home Design*, 2012.

Brusco, Sam. *Rhode Island Home & Design Magazine.* I had a monthly column called "Contractor Truths" until the magazine went out of business. I cited many of my own remodeling projects as examples.

Deep River Partners, Ltd.

Perspectives on Design Great Lakes. Plano, TX: Panache Partners, LLC, 2010.

Rooney, E. Ashley. *Today's Historic Interiors.* Atglen, PA: Schiffer Publishing, Ltd., 2011.

Conner, Lori. "Well Traveled," *Luxe, The Chicago Home Redefined,* Sandow Media LLC Volume III, Issue II, pp. 164-175.

Conner, Lori. "Dream Catchers," *Arts and Crafts Homes and the Revival.* Gloucester, MA: Gloucester Publishers, Volume III, Number 3, pp. 64-69.

Perspectives on Design Great Lakes. Plano, TX: Panache Partners, LLC, 2010.

Rooney, E. Ashley. *Today's Historic Interiors.* Atglen PA: Schiffer Publishing, Ltd., 2011.

Diane Gordy

Karth, Barbara. "City Living," *Home & Design,* September/October 2009.

McKeon, Nancy. "Dumbarton Oaks," *The Washington Post. At Home.* Spring 2009.

Lifestyle Interior Design

"Deep Soak." *The Denver Post,* April 28, 2008.

"Profile of Sandra Clinger," *Architecture & Design of the West,* Summer 2008.

"Ranch Revival a la Sandra Clinger," *Colorado Expression,* October/November 2008.

Brewster, Janice. *Cabin Decor Ideas*. Lincolnwood, IL: Publications International Ltd., 2004.

Brewster, Janice. "Back to the Land," *Cabin Style,* Lincolnwood, IL: Publications International Ltd., 2001.

Colorado Expressions. *Christmas in Colorado.* Denver, CO: Westcliff Pub Inc., 2008.

Clements Park Renovation. *Colorado Expression*, June/July 2008.

Designer Q&A. *Colorado Homes & Lifestyles Magazine*, October 2001.

Frederick, Lisa Gaddy. "Reliving History," *Better Homes and Gardens,* Des Moines, Iowa, 2004.

Fulweiler, Megan. "Tasteful Traditional," *Ultimate Decorating,* Lincolnwood, IL: Publications International Ltd., 2003.

"Hot Baths!" *Colorado Homes & Lifestyles*, March 2001.

"Keep on Truckin'," *Colorado Homes & Lifestyles*, November/December 2001.

"Mastering the Bath," *Colorado Homes & Lifestyles*, March 2001.

Overbeck, Joy. "Architecture and Design of the West," *Colorado Expression*, 2008.

Rooney, E. Ashley. *Today's Historic Interiors*. Atglen, Pa: Schiffer Publishing, Ltd., 2011.

"The Bedroom/Bath Experience: Your Buyers' Private Refuge. Ideas, Sales, and Marketing," January 2004.

Vitale, Terry. *Christmas in Colorado*. Denver, CO: New West Publishing, 2008.
"Wow Factors for Clients Over 50," *Custom Builder,* April 2009.

LifeWise Renovations

Bontrager, Katherine. "Renovating a Home, Empowering a Life," *Leawood Lifestyle*, November 2011.
Friedel, Linda. "Nurses' Healthcare Vision Crosses Company And World," *Kansas City Nursing News*, February 6, 2011.
Kellogg, Gina. "There's No Place Like Home," *Enhance Magazine*, September/October 2011.
Murphy, Kevin. "Boom Times," *Thinking Bigger Business,* April 2012.
Stafford, Diane. "Growing Older in Kansas City," *Kansas City Star*, April 2011.

Honors

Kansas City, Smart Companies to Watch 2011. Awarded by *Small Business Monthly.*

Jill Hertz Interior Design—Leslie Shankman-Cohn

Liao, Alice. "Heightened Awareness: A thoughtful kitchen remodel puts design within reach," *K+BB*, September 2008.
Van Sickle, Suzi. "Little Woman, Big Kitchen," *MIDSOUTH Magazine*, September 2008.
Wiedower, Stacey. "The Appeal: One Design Fits All," *Home and Garden*, November 25, 2011.

Honors

ASID, TN. Designer of the Year, 2005.
ASID, TN. Kenneth C Kimbrough Award of Excellence, 2006.
National Homebuilder's Association, Homes for Life Award. Single Space; Universal Design Kitchen, 2008.
ASID ICON. A Universally Designed Kitchen, November 2008.
The Commercial Appeal. "Leslie Shankman-Cohn wins Homes for Life Award," November 2008.
ASID TN CHAPTER, Residential Singular Space. Silver Award, 2008.

Neville Gerald Architects, formerly Neville Architecture

Carter, Rachel. "The Sun Spot," *Newport Life Magazine's* Home and Lifestyle Issue, 2009.
Mitchell, Ellen. "Born-Again Barns," *New York Newsday's* Real Estate Cover Story, 2002.
Rooney, E. Ashley. *Barn Again Residential Conversions*. Atglen, PA: Schiffer Publishing Ltd., 2010.

Honorable Mention

Constructive Ideas Competition for an Urban Corridor. Sponsored by the Baltimore Foundation. Featured in *Baltimore Sun* and exhibited at Maryland Art Place.

Perianth Interior Design/Buy My Eye®—Hiliary Unger
Caldwell, Andrew. "Art Apartment," *Memphis Flyer*, 2011.
"Chasing Your Design Dreams With Hilary Unger," *Freshome,* 2010.
Conti, Teegan. "Turning Everyday Space into a Personal Sanctuary," *The New York Observer,* 2010.
Derringer, Jaime. "The Ultimate Boys' Bedroom," *ShelterPop,* 2010.
"Discover: Interior Designers on Vedere Pay Tribute to Renowned Decorator Albert Hadley," *Vedere,* 2012.
"Fifth Avenue Apartment," *RAENOVATE*, 2010.
King, Andrika. "Boys Loft Spaces on Nesting Newbies," *Nursery Notations*, 2010.
Mann About Town. "The Perfect Family Kitchen for the Kosher Lifestyle," *Mann Publications,* 2010.
Mann Report Building. "Interior Design is a Household Word...And So Too Is 'Buy My Eye'," *Mann Publications*, 2011.
McKeough, Tim. "The Art of E-Design," *Elle Décor*, 2011.
Nook. "Find Function and Beauty in obscure places," *Nesting Newbies Magazine*, 2010.
"NYC Home Office," *RAENOVATE*, 2012.
Priluck, Jill. "Room to Grow," *The Wall Street Journal*, 2010.
Trover, Sarah Rae. "Before & After: Clunky Colonial to Caribbean Cool," *Apartment Therapy,* 2010.
Durand, Faith. "Creating a Kosher Kitchen," *Apartment Therapy*, 2010.
Rich, Laura. "Making Your Home into Your Office," *Recessionwire,* 2009.
"Riverside Drive Apartment," *RAENOVATE*, 2011.
Runyon, M. Carolyn. "A Place for Everything," *Your Home and Lifestyle*, 2011.
Runyon, M. Carolyn. "Master of Illusion," *Your Home and Lifestyle*, 2011.
Vedere Blog. "V Trends: Talented Interior Designers Jump On The Wallpaper Bandwagon," *Vedere*, 2012.
Runyon, M. Carolyn. "Work of Art," *Your Home and Lifestyle*, 2012.
Scelfo, Julie. "The $300 Makeover: West Village Studio," *The New York Times,* 2009.
Unger, Hilary. "Storage and More: Ideas for Kid's Rooms," *Whistle and Wink*, 2010.

Peter Brock, Architect
Barnes, Christine. *Before and After Baths.* Tampa, FL: Sunset Books, 2006.
Fine Homebuilding Great Houses. *Timber Frame Houses.* Newtown, CT: Taunton Press, 1992.
Rooney, E. Ashley. *Cliffhangers & Hillside Houses.* Atglen, PA: Schiffer Publishing, Ltd., 2006.
Thomas, Steve and Phillip Langdon. *This Old House Bathrooms: A Guide to Design and Renovation.* New York, NY: Little Brown & Company, 1993.

Thomas, Steve and Phillip Langdon. *This Old House Kitchens: A Guide to Design and Renovation*. New York, NY: Little Brown & Company, 1992.

S. Barzin Architect

"Kitchen Highlights on the Bay. A workplace that gleams," *Fine Homebuildings*, Kitchen & Baths Annual Issue, 2002.

Bouknight, Joanne Keller. *New Kitchen Idea Book*. Newtown, CT: Taunton Press, 2004.

Honors

RI Monthly Design Award, 2008 Bronze Award.

Thielsen Architects

Drueding, Meghan. "Light Construction," *Custom Home,* January/February 2007.

"Lakefront Home," *Homes Across America,* HGTV, April 18, 2005.

Masredjian, Luci. "Joyous Renovation," *Seattle Homes and Lifestyles,* December 2007.

"The Maine Course," *Seattle Homes and Lifestyles,* May 2004.

Thompson Naylor Architects

Katz, Barry. *Practical Green Remodeling: Down to Earth Solutions for Everyday Homes*. Newtown, CT: The Taunton Press, Inc., 2010.

Rooney, E. Ashley. *Green Homes—Dwellings for the 21st Century*. Atglen, PA: Schiffer Publishing, Ltd. June 2008.

Honors

Recipients of the Santa Barbara County "Green Award," recognizing exceptional environmental businesses, 2001.

Nominated for California Council, A.I.A., "Community Housing Assistance" Award, 1991.

RESOURCES

Leading the building industry in the Santa Barbara and Ventura County region of California for three decades, **Allen Associates**, the project general contractor, excels in constructing small remodels of large custom homes. The employee-owned company is nationally recognized for its professionalism, artistry, competitive pricing, and leadership in the sustainable building movement.

Allen Associates
201 N. Milpas St.
Santa Barbara, CA 93103
http://www.dennisallenassociates.com
bhenson@dallenassoc.com

Dr. Jill M. Bjerke is the founder and president of **Cut the Clutter Company, LLC** and its division, **Aging in Place with Grace**. Cut the Clutter focuses on customized solutions and services for those wishing to reorganize, downsize, eliminate clutter, and create clean and simple living spaces. As a Certified Aging in Place Specialist (CAPS), she created Aging in Place with Grace as a source of information and services for those who need support in determining if staying in their own homes as they age is the right decision for them. To this end, she has a created a home assessment software program to be released in 2012 that will provide builders, remodelers, occupational and physical therapists, and senior service providers with a tool to help determine the changes a residence needs to make it "age in place" friendly and safe. She is a health care physician, international author, and much sought-after speaker, and she was just appointed to the Iowa State Commission on Aging.

www.AgingInPlaceWithGrace.com
www.CutTheClutterCo.com
CutTheClutterCo@gmail.com

Brion Jeannette Architecture began energizing the lives of its clients via creative residential design in the early 1970s. The firm's work reflects unique and varied architectural styles shaped not only by their clients' aesthetic preferences and expectations, but site potential, natural light, and energy conservation principles as well. Their commissions include hundreds of private homes and estates, most prominently on the southern California coast. Many have earned worldwide acclaim, resulting in international work. The firm is noted for employing cutting-edge techniques and technologies in every home, large or small. Their understanding and tenacity in securing precedent-setting approvals through complex governing agencies is a testimony to the dedication with which they approach their work.

Brion Jeannette Architecture
470 Old Newport Blvd.
Newport Beach, CA 92663
www.customarchitecture.com

Brock Rubina Architects is a collaboration of architects and craftspeople in Berkeley, California, and Princeton, New Jersey. Working together for over a decade, we have been making buildings, furniture, and objects of art to meet the needs of diverse clients across a wide spectrum of project scale, geographic setting, and stylistic context. The firm's creative and collaborative approach to design allows it to work closely with clients, design professionals, builders, and others who care deeply about their work and take pride in their craft. It prides itself on its thoughtful and innovative solutions to all design problems.

Peter Brock, Architect
28 Quarry Street
Princeton, NJ 08542

Marina Rubina, Architect
812 Camelia Street
Berkeley, CA 94710
www.mrubina.com
www.peter-brock.com

Founded in 2002, **Brusco Design & Renovation** is a full-service remodeling company that shows their clients what they will get before the first hammer is swung. They are members of the National Association of the Remodeling Industry (NARI) and the National Association of Home Builders (NAHB). Sam Brusco holds several certifications including Certified Aging in Place Specialist (CAPS was codeveloped with the AARP), Certified Active Adult Housing Specialist (for the 50+

homeowners), Certified Green Professional (CGP is similar to LEED AP for Homes) and Certified Graduate Remodeler (CGR). Brusco is also a former writer for *Rhode Island Home & Design Magazine*, where he had a monthly column called "Contractor Truths." Since 2008, Brusco has been teaching homeowners "How to Avoid a Renovation Horror" for Rhode Island public libraries.

Brusco Design & Renovation
11 Alhambra Circle
Cranston, RI 02905
www.BruscoDesign.com
Sam@BruscoDesign.com

Roxane Carson CAPS is an independent contractor specializing in aging in place. She has a Bachelors of Science degree in interior design from Brown College. She is a member of the National Aging In Place Council and also her local Minneapolis/St. Paul Chapter of Aging in Place. She designs kitchens and baths primarily and has experience and passion for the elderly, helping to keep them in their own homes, where they want to be.

Roxane Carson
14350 Ebony Lane
Apple Valley, MN 55124
www.roxanecarsondesigns.com
roxanecarson@juno.com

Sandra Elizabeth Clinger, MA, Allied ASID, CAASH, is President of **Lifestyle Interior Design**, an international interior design and model home merchandising firm. Ms. Clinger is a popular project manager, consulting with custom home clients and builders on interior and exterior specifications and purchasing.

Her work is featured in over fifty publications, including *Ultimate Decorating and Cabin Style* by Publications International and *Today's Historic Interiors* by Schiffer Publishing. Ms. Clinger is the first place recipient of numerous design awards, including the IDA Award, the CARE Award, the coveted National ASID Design Specialty Award for Historic Preservation, and the Colorado Homes & Lifestyles Magazine Home of the Year Award. As early as 2001, Ms. Clinger received a Special

Recognition Award from the American Society of Interior Designers, Colorado Chapter, for her work in aging in place.

Lifestyle Interior Design
www.lifestyleinteriordesign.com
lifestyle@ecentral.com

Carolyn Cook, LEED AP ID+C, CAPS, has been a healthcare interior designer for twenty-one years. LEED accredited, she designed the interiors for the first certified LEED Silver apartment building in Charlotte, North Carolina. She is an advocate for affordable Senior Housing, a proponent for Universal Design and is a Certified Aging-in-Place Specialist. Carolyn presents to senior organizations, community groups, and industry professionals on the topic of universal design. She also developed and taught an aging in place course for the Central Piedmont Community College in Charlotte. In 2009, Carolyn combined her passions for sustainability, healthcare, and universal design to form her company **LiveSmart Design.** Specializing in the design of kitchens and bathrooms, Carolyn's goal is to help people remain safely in their homes for as long as they choose, regardless of their age or ability. She addresses accessibility in the home by working under the existing roofline and believes strongly that adding more rooms is not always the answer.

LiveSmart Design
Charlotte, NC 28205
www.livesmartdesign.com
carolyn@livesmartdesign.com

Deep River Partners, Ltd. specializes in residential design including renovation/remodeling, new homes, historic renovation, and condominium build-outs. "Our award-winning architects and interior designers provide a holistic design process that produces creative and personalized solutions reflecting our clients' vision. Through the integration of architecture, interiors, lighting, mechanical systems, and product selection, we create environments that encourage people to flourish. Our services include project assessment, architectural and interior design, construction documents, competitive bidding, and construction administration."

Deep River Partners, Ltd.
338 North Milwaukee St., Suite 505
Milwaukee, WI 53202
www.deep-river.com
rsherer@deep-river.com

Mike Dodd, MCR, CKBR, GCP, CAPS has been a leader in the remodeling industry for twenty-five years. He launched **LifeWise Renovations** in 2009 to focus on his passion of helping individuals remain in their home, the place they love the most. Mike and his team of project managers and occupational therapists work closely with their clients in order to make their homes as safe and functional as possible. They specialize in kitchens, bathrooms, and room additions, and have recently launched a Welcome Home© package aimed specifically at the health care community to assist in transitioning clients from the care setting to home. Mike and his cohorts bring intelligence not only from the remodeling side, but from the home health side as well. Their collective expertise in delivery systems and solutions enhances LifeWise's focus on providing customized modifications that allow their clients to remain where they can be happiest and healthiest.

LifeWise Renovations
3500 W. 75th St. Suite 100
Prairie Village, KS 66208
lifewiserenovations.com
mdodd@lifewiserenovations.com

As principal and design director of the award-winning **Diane Gordy Interiors**, Diane Gordy, M Arch, has practiced as a leading interior designer, new construction planner and manager, and renovation consultant conceiving and executing built environments from inception to installation in over 500 light commercial and residential design projects throughout the Eastern Seaboard, Southern California, and abroad for thirty years. Diane Gordy Interiors offers interior architecture, interior design, and interior decoration services with a concentration on luxury renovation, green design, designing for life-changes, and universal design.

As former Chair of the Maryland State Board of Interior Designers and former chair of the Maryland Coalition of Interior Designers, Gordy was an active leader in the Washington Metro Chapter of the American Society of Interior Designers (ASID), a Legislative Liaison and Government and Public Affairs team leader, and has served ASID National on the International Advisory Council.

Diane Gordy Interiors
179 Main Street
Palm Beach, FL 33480
www.dianegordy.com
dgordy@cs.net

For over 25 years, **Green Construction Services, Inc.** has been serving Central Florida as a full-service construction company specializing in restoration and remodeling. Their Certified Aging in Place Specialists (CAPS) have received national recognition for their design/build projects utilizing universal design. Their hands-on management philosophy allows them to work closely with their clients, keeping them intimately involved and up-to-date through every step up the construction project.

Green Construction Services, Inc.
2525 Drane Field Rd., Suite 13
Lakeland, FL 33811
www.green-construction.com
dean@green-construction.com

Stephen Hatcher developed numerous cutting-edge devices for the wireless communications industry. Retiring from this field in 2000, he returned to art through his interests in wood turning and stone carving. Merging these techniques led to his unique style of artwork. His art is collected here and in Canada and has been presented in numerous publications.

Stephen Hatcher
summitdesign@comcast.net

MBC Building & Remodeling, LLC (MBC) began changing the lives of Lancaster County, Pennsylvania, residents in 1999. Combining an extensive knowledge of the remodeling process and a passion for building beautiful spaces for his clients, Mike Blank, CGR CAPS, has led MBC into the present day by sticking to his vision. As a full-service remodeling company, MBC offers a variety of home improvement options, leaving the client without any hassles.

MBC Building & Remodeling LLC
PO Box 53
Millersville, PA 17551
www.MBCremodeling.com
Mike@MBCremodeling.com

Naomi Neville, principal of **Neville Gerald Architects, formerly Neville Architecture**, is a registered architect in California, Massachusetts, New York, and Rhode Island, and a LEED AP. She has taught a LEED preparatory course tailored for other professionals in the engineering and architectural professions. Over the last fifteen years, she has designed and built commercial, multi-use, and residential projects. Each project is designed with an understanding of the local environment, the global environment, its historic context, and long-term goals for success.
Naomi has a BA from Yale University and a Master in Architecture from Columbia University, where she received a William Kinney Memorial Fellowship. She was also a recipient of the *Providence Business News* 40 Under 40 Award, given to outstanding individuals in the Rhode Island business community.

Neville Gerald Architects
11A Bridge Street
Newport, RI 02840
www.NGArchitects.com
Office@NGArchitects.com

Patrick's Residential Management Services
Custom-made cabinets and interior renovation projects add comfort and style to any home. Patrick's offers kitchens, bathrooms, and all interior work with help from planning process to installation.

Patrick McGrath
16 Mann Avenue
Newport RI 02840
www.patricksri.com
Patrick@patricksri.com

Peter Brock, Architect, is a group of architects and craftspeople in Berkeley, California. For over twenty-five years, the firm has been making buildings, furniture, and objects of art to meet the needs of diverse clients across a wide spectrum of project scale, geographic setting, and stylistic context. The firm thrives on close collaborations with owners and artisans engaged in solving unique design challenges with craftsmanship and creative and responsible use of natural materials.

Peter Brock, Architect
812 Camelia St.
Berkeley, CA 94710
www.peter-brock.com

Pineapple House Interior Design is a celebrated interior design and architectural specification firm that offers turnkey design and orchestration of residential interiors. Innovative, award-winning experts handle any aspect of the process, from the decoration of an existing home to the construction of a new one. Pineapple House designers work nationally and internationally in a variety of design styles.

Pineapple House Interior Design
190 Ottley Drive
Atlanta, GA 30324
www.pineapplehouse.com
info@pineapplehouse.com

Based in Newport, Rhode Island, **PLACEstudio** specializes in designs for private residences and commercial and institutional clients. Designing the landscape is a team collaboration between the designer, the client, and the builder. **PLACEstudio** designs distinctive landscapes that respond to the existing cultural and natural contexts of the site, always seeking to find the balance between man and nature, the traditional and the new.

Founder Tanya Kelley received a Master's in Landscape Architecture from the Rhode Island School of Design in 2001 and a Bachelor's Degree in Urban Landscape Architecture from the City College of The City of New York in 1999.

PLACEstudio landscape design
1 Stone St.
Newport, RI 02840

Founded in 2006, **RED Interior** offers full-service design capabilities for new construction, remodels, and home furnishings in the greater San Diego, California, area. Certified interior designer, Rebecca Soechtig, ASID, CID, CAP owns and operates this custom design firm, which creates timeless, original designs based on the architecture of the home and the unique desires and lifestyle needs of each client. As an AARP-endorsed CAPS design firm, RED Interior approaches the design process with a fresh perspective, listening to the needs of each individual client and then pushing the proverbial envelope to create practical living spaces with astonishing beauty.

RED Interior
7527 Girard Ave.
La Jolla, CA 92037
www.redinterior.com
mail@redinterior.com

S. Barzin Architect (SBA) is a full service architecture and design firm in Jamestown, RI, founded by architect Shahin Barzin, AIA, CAPS. SBA designs are noted for their elegance, craftsmanship, and practicality. We approach the design with the understanding that every project is unique in relation to the client's needs and the site characteristics. Our primary objective is to understand the client's needs and expectations and how to foster their vision into reality. Projects range from beachfront houses to simple straw bale homes, medical offices, and "Green" LEED certifiable office buildings. The firm has a special branch, "Aging Comforts" with the focus on custom design homes for the physically disabled with needed amenities as well as residences with universal design concepts adequate for aging in place.

S. Barzin Architect
PO Box 633
Jamestown, RI 02835
www.SbarzinArchitect.com
Info@SbarzinArchitect.com

Leslie Shankman-Cohn, ASID, CAPS, CGP, is a partner in the firm of **Jill Hertz Interior Design (JHID)**, which specializes in high-end residential interior design, new construction, remodeling, kitchen and bath design, cabinetry, custom tile design, and lighting. The designers of JHID have been the recipients of many design awards and honors. She is a Past-President of the Tennessee Chapter of ASID, a past board member of the Tennessee Interior Design Coalition, served on ASID's national committee on "Aging in Place," and involved in "Redesigning for an Aging America," a local consortium focusing the future of Memphis' city planning and social services. The governor of Tennessee appointed Leslie as the Interior Design representative on the Board of Architectural and Engineering Examiners for the State of Tennessee, where she will serve until the end of 2012. In addition, she is the Tennessee Delegate to the NCIDQ National Board. Leslie is the recipient of the 2006 Kenneth C. Kimbrough Award of Excellence by the Tennessee Chapter of ASID and the chapter's 2005 Designer of the Year. Among her many other awards, she is most proud of The National Homebuilder's Association 2008 National "Homes for Life" design award for a kitchen she designed utilizing universal design and sustainable design components. She has written for many different publications and lectured various groups throughout the nation.

Jill Hertz Interior Design
710 S. Perkins Rd
Memphis, TN 38117
www.jillhertz.com

Thielsen Architects is a vibrant design-oriented firm that is committed to creating distinctive built environments. Their clients become integral members of the design team, allowing their individual needs and desires to shape the project direction. Thoughtful spatial organization, in conjunction with sensitivity to the individual site, allows Thielsen Architects to provide clear, sensible design solutions for their projects. Building forms and interior spaces are defined by an integrated interior and exterior architecture that is responsive to the site, local climate, and seasonal changes in natural light. They design architecture that is not only functional and beautiful today, but will remain so over time.

Thielsen Architects
720 Market Street, Suite C
Kirkland, WA 98033
www.thielsen.com
inquiries@thielsen.com

Susette Naylor and Dennis Thompson have worked together since 1985. Their firm, **Thompson-Naylor Architects**, practices "Socially and Environmentally Responsible Architecture and Planning" in Santa Barbara. In addition to custom homes, Susette and Dennis have designed affordable housing, spiritual buildings, and schools. Their work has won numerous design awards and has been published frequently. They are most proud of their commitment to "green building" and their long-term relationships with many former clients.

Thompson-Naylor Architects
900 Philinda Ave.
Santa Barbara, CA 93103
www.thompsonnaylor.com

Hilary Unger of **Buy My Eye®** says, "My work as an interior designer has always been meaningful to me. It gives me the opportunity to improve people's surroundings, which ultimately improves their quality of life. Since I was young, I've always been affected by my physical environment with regard to light, organization, and general feel of the space around me. When things are in order, there is a peacefulness that follows. Chaos and disorder can create stress. I'm acutely aware that our surroundings provoke various emotions, and I bear that in mind when I work with my clients.

"In all of my designs, my goal is to address my clients' most needed "functions" first, and as such, we begin with the basics: what will the space be used for? In the case of aging in place, one must address the needs of the client even more specifically than in a typical home. Once this functionality is addressed, then the beauty of the environment can be addressed, incorporating color, fabrics, and textures. My philosophy is that our design plan must translate visually into what the client is hoping to convey, and it's my job to make their wishes come true (in the most tasteful way!).

"When I first meet with a client, I immediately get a sense of them, their aesthetic, their ideal physical environment, and what is important to them from an ergonomic perspective. An important element I'm always careful to bear in mind is that the design is not about me. It is about the client and what they want, what is important to them and how they want to live. I just bring my level of expertise to whatever look is desired.

"Regardless of our income level and the square footage we have to work with, we all want to live in a peaceful, functional, wonderful home. With my two companies, Perianth Interior Design and Buy My Eye, I aim to help people attain their level of comfort and create beauty at the same time. With sixteen years of experience, I stand by my track record of delivering on that."

Buy My Eye®
Interior Design Services at a Glance
204 West 84th St. 3rd Floor
New York, New NY 10024
www.perianth.com
www.buymyeye.net
maca@perianth.com

INDEX